# CULTURES OF THE WORLD®

# IRELAND

*Patricia Levy*

**BENCHMARK BOOKS**

MARSHALL CAVENDISH
NEW YORK

**PICTURE CREDITS**

Cover photo: © Art Directors/Jean Hall

AFP: 41 • APA: 22, 47, 65, 67, 68, 71, 73, 80, 89, 95, 96, 105, 121 • Bes Stock: 6 • Alain Le Garsmeur / CORBIS: 53 • Geray Sweeney / CORBIS: 112 • Michael St. Maur Sheil / CORBIS: 94 • Tim De Waele / CORBIS: 107 • Tim Thompson / CORBIS: 58 • Corel: 51 • David Simson: 16, 62, 64, 92, 117 • Dylan Garcia / Still Pictures: 52 • Eye Ubiquitous / Hugh Rooney: 78 • Eye Ubiquitous / Tim Page: 106 • Focus: 5, 57, 66, 86, 104, 120 • Hulton-Deutsch: 23, 24, 28, 29, 30, 31, 32, 33, 99, 101 • The Hutchison Library: 10, 35, 37, 40, 46, 54, 60, 70, 76, 85, 102, 109, 115, 124 • Image Bank: 4, 9, 11, 12, 13, 43, 44, 59, 61, 74, 93, 125 • International Photobank: 8, 50 • James Davis Worldwide: 18, 34 • Kay Shaw Photography: 1 • Life File Photo Library: 19, 21, 72, 77, 79, 81, 82, 83, 87, 103, 108, 116, 119, 122, 128 • Life File Photo Library: 3 • Lonely Planet Images: 130 • Lynelle Seow: 131 • Northern Ireland Tourist Board: 7, 14, 15, 38, 48, 49, 75, 98, 100, 111, 113, 126, 127 • Photo Disc: 55, 56 • The Slide File: 114 • Travel Ink: 42

**ACKNOWLEDGMENTS**

Thanks to Professor Catherine McKenna of the Graduate Center at the City University of New York for her expert reading of this manuscript.

**PRECEDING PAGE**

A group of schoolboys on an excursion to the Fota Wildlife Park in County Cork.

Marshall Cavendish Benchmark
99 White Plains Road
Tarrytown, NY 10591
Website: www.marshallcavendish.us

© Times Media Private Limited 1996, 1994
© Marshall Cavendish International (Asia) Private Limited 2004
All rights reserved. First edition 1994. Second edition 2004.

® "Cultures of the World" is a registered trademark of Marshall Cavendish Corporation.

Originated and designed by Times Books International
An imprint of Marshall Cavendish International (Asia) Private Limited
A member of Times Publishing Limited

*Library of Congress Cataloging-in-Publication Data*
Levy, Patricia, 1951-
Ireland / Patricia Levy.— 2nd ed.
   p. cm. — (Cultures of the world)
Includes bibliographical references and index.
   ISBN 0-7614-1784-2
1. Ireland—Juvenile literature. I. Title.
DA906.L48 2005
941.5—dc22                         2004012902

Printed in China

7 6 5 4 3 2

# CONTENTS

A red-headed Irish girl.

3

A stone carving from one of Ireland's early Christian churches.

# INTRODUCTION

SITUATED ON THE FARTHEST WESTERN EDGE OF EUROPE, Ireland is an island of green pastures, warm rains, and a rich and diverse history. Ireland's cities are small but very much a part of 21st-century Europe, while its rural areas still remember a traditional and ancient way of life. Ireland is also a land of contradictions: Northern Ireland has been one of the world's most volatile trouble spots, while the Republic of Ireland is one of the safest, most peaceful places to live in the world.

This book looks at Ireland and the Irish: their work, in the fields and in the large multinational firms now so crucial to the country's economy; their pastimes, from lively conversations to soccer and a night out at the pub; their culture, so rich and diverse in its language, music, and remarkable literary tradition; and their beliefs, deeply rooted in their faith. It offers glimpses and insights into a country with more to it than the leprechauns and shamrocks that many outsiders associate with the country.

# GEOGRAPHY

IRELAND IS TUCKED AWAY in the far west of Europe, battered by Atlantic gales but warmed by the North Atlantic Current. It is surrounded by the sea and deluged by warm ocean rains.

Its land area of 32,592 square miles (84,412 square km) consists largely of pasture and agricultural land. Ireland's rainy climate is perfect for pasture and root crops. Much of Ireland consists of raised bog. This is useless for agriculture but provides peat, a form of fuel.

The country consists of a central plain surrounded by a broken ring of mountains. In the east are the Wicklow Mountains. In the south are the broken ranges of Cork and Kerry with the highest peak in Ireland, Carrantouhill, standing at 3,415 feet (1,041 m). The central plain is drained to the west by the mighty River Shannon, while to the northeast, Lough (LOK) Neagh is the largest lake in the British Isles. Along the west coast are scattered many small islands inhabited by seafaring people.

*Left:* **The River Bann in Northern Ireland.**

*Opposite:* **The village of Glandore in County Cork has a mild climate as it is located along the path of the North Atlantic Current.**

## THE RAISED BOG

Ireland's central plain was formed with a base of boulder clay. Water accumulated on the clay, forming lakes. At the edges marshes developed and these encroached into the lake. As the plants died they fell into the lake, and over time they became blocked with plant matter until only bog mosses and plants that could survive on the nutrients in rainwater remained.

These bog plants turned into peat, and the raised bog came into existence. Bogs have provided fuel for millions of Irish families over centuries. In recent years, the commercial exploitation of these bogs has depleted them, and soon, few will remain.

The Kerry Bog Museum in County Kerry, where visitors see peat being harvested from bogs.

## *CLIMATE*

Ireland's geographical location determines its weather patterns. It has a maritime climate with uniform temperatures across the country. Far away in the Gulf of Mexico, tropical temperatures heat the seawater that flows through the Florida Straits and becomes the Gulf Stream. An offshoot of the stream, the North Atlantic Current, brings warm waters and huge rainclouds to the western coast of Ireland.

Ireland rarely experiences 24 hours of frost, even in the center of the country where the maritime influence is less and temperatures are lower. In the warmest months of July and August, temperatures occasionally rise above 61°F (16°C). Heavy cloud cover for most of the year keeps temperatures low in summer and above freezing in winter.

Ireland experiences an average of between 2 and 3 inches (51 and 76 mm) of rainfall a month, most of it falling as a gentle mist.

In the west of Ireland the coastline is subject to fierce Atlantic storms that often reach hurricane force and are capable of doing considerable damage to buildings and infrastructure.

Ireland often experiences high winds with gusts of up to 80 miles per hour (129 km per hour). The winds can also make Ireland's rocky coastline a dangerous place to be. Every year people are reported lost at sea.

**Slieve Mish Mountains, County Kerry.**

## LANDSCAPES

**THE WICKLOW MOUNTAINS** Stretching in a broken line for 40 miles (64 km) from Dublin southward to Wexford, the Wicklow Mountains are a series of granite peaks covered by a surface layer of peat bog. The mountains are broken up by deep rifts cut by rivers that descend from the mountains.

The Wicklow Mountains are a haven for wildlife, just as they were once a haven for rebels who attacked the English settlers to take their crops. Despite their modest height, the mountains are sparsely populated and many of the hillsides are used for forestry projects. Ireland's trees were virtually wiped out from the 16th century onward. Today, nearly 70,000 acres (28,100 hectares) are devoted to forestry projects in the Wicklow region alone.

**THE MOUNTAINS OF CORK AND KERRY** Southwestern Ireland is broken up by many mountain ranges. None of these are high by European standards, but they create an area of outstanding beauty and make the counties of Cork and Kerry major attractions for visitors. Chiefly made of old red sandstone deposited by raging rivers millions of years ago and then thrust up by movements of the earth, these mountains were gradually cut and worn smooth by the movements of glaciers. This is cattle-rearing territory, with few fields of grain or other crops. The typical Irish farmer in this area has a small farm of tens of acres and rears cattle. A local creamery collects milk daily from the farmer. Everything is small-scale.

Three conspicuous mountain ranges extend into the sea along the three peninsulas of west Cork and Kerry. The Slieve Mish Mountains form the backbone of the Dingle Peninsula; Macgillycuddy's Reeks with the towering Carrantouhill jut out along the Iveragh Peninsula; and the Beara Peninsula is home to the Caha and Slieve Miskish mountains. At their extreme edges these wild and alien peninsulas consist of bare rock, with small farms and trees clinging to the windblown surface.

A curragh (traditional fishing craft) being carried from the sea at Inisheer, one of the Aran Islands.

**IRELAND'S ISLANDS** Off the western coast of Ireland are many smaller islands whose inhabitants batten down for the long windy winters, farm the hard lands, and cater to the increasing numbers of tourists during the summer.

The Aran Islands are the most well known of the islands. They consist of three limestone islands—Inishmore, Inishmaan, and Inisheer—lying in the mouth of Galway Bay, with the sea cutting them off from the mainland for part of the winter. The largest of the islands, Inishmore, is 8 miles (13 km) long by 2 miles (3 km) wide. The islands are linked geologically to the Burren, an area of County Clare to their south. Tiny fields are enclosed by walls whose function is to make use of the rocks rather than to mark a boundary. The islands' inhabitants scrape a bare living from these fields and the sea. The Aran Islands are one of the few places where Gaelic is still spoken.

## THE GIANT'S CAUSEWAY

On the coast of Antrim in Northern Ireland is a strange cliff area known as the Giant's Causeway. It consists of hundreds of hexagonal pillars of basalt rock stacked up neatly and forming what looks like a giant's pathway disappearing out to sea in the direction of Scotland. In times past, this pathway extended all the way to the Scottish coast where the other end of it can still be seen today.

# THE CITIES OF IRELAND

Compared to cities in the rest of Europe, Ireland's major centers are small, friendly places where the tempo is perhaps a little faster than the slow pace of rural Irish life.

**DUBLIN**  Even though it is the capital city of the Republic of Ireland, Dublin is still small enough for its inhabitants to be familiar with all of its streets. Due to poor planning in the 1950s Dublin's inner city has suffered from urban decay, and until the urban regeneration programs of the 1990s, most people lived outside the city in satellite towns.

Grafton Street in the center of Dublin on a busy summer day.

Nevertheless, planners avoided high-rise buildings, so there are no skyscrapers in Dublin. One building, the Central Bank on Dame Street, exceeded the city's height limits and had to be lowered by its builders. Dublin is the country's business center, and many of its inhabitants are white-collar workers and civil servants. It sits at the intersection of the River Liffey and the Irish Sea and is a major trading port and sea passenger link with Britain. Its population is less than 1 million.

**CORK**  The county seat and the second largest city in the Republic of Ireland, Cork is located on the southern coast and is small enough for the visitor to feel at home very quickly. Like Dublin, it became important because of its sea links and river system. It was once a great mercantile center, and visitors to its main streets can see the remains of great warehouses and quaysides.

City Hall in Belfast.

**BELFAST** Much more industrial in appearance than other Irish cities, Belfast has regularly featured in world news because of the civil unrest there, caused by the opposing factions of nationalist and loyalist supporters. The city's housing estates are clearly marked out into Protestant and Catholic areas, and armored cars can be seen carrying heavily armed police and British soldiers wearing bulletproof vests. Despite this, the city's inhabitants carry on with life normally. Its chief industries are engineering, shipbuilding, linen manufacture, and food processing.

**DERRY** Known in Britain as Londonderry and in Dublin as Derry, even the name of this city is in dispute. It sits in Northern Ireland near the border with the Republic of Ireland and has seen many civil disturbances in recent decades. A museum of Derry's complex history now graces one section of its old city wall, while international hotels and stylish restaurants are found on the other side of the wall. Its chief industries are engineering, textiles, chemical processing, and ceramics.

# FLORA AND FAUNA

Between 40,000 and 13,000 years ago, the flora and fauna of Ireland were considerably different from today. Remains have been found of woolly mammoths, brown bears, spotted hyenas, wolves, arctic foxes, and giant Irish deer, as well as smaller creatures such as lemmings. The last Ice Age saw the end of most of these exotic creatures, but Ireland still provides a home—at least for part of the year—to many endangered species. One of these is the Greenland white-fronted goose, which migrates to Ireland during the winter months and finds a safe roosting site in the bogland. Although the Irish bogs are under threat of extinction, some are now protected. This means that the geese, along with several other rare plants and animals, are safe there for now.

**Kingfishers thrive in Ireland's unspoiled countryside.**

More common wildlife found in Ireland are badgers, hares, rabbits, stoats, and minks. Otters, now quite rare in other parts of Europe, thrive in Ireland. The country has fewer species of both plants and animals than Britain—evidence that the repopulation of Ireland after the last Ice Age was delayed because the land link between Ireland and mainland Britain had disappeared by that time. However, the presence in Ireland of some Mediterranean-type plants that do not exist in Britain suggests that there was a land link with Europe still in existence. One such plant is the strawberry tree, not native to Britain but common to parts of Kerry and the Mediterranean. Other plants similarly common in Ireland but rare or nonexistent in Britain are Irish spurge, a poisonous plant; the Kerry lily, rare even in Ireland; the greater butterwort, a tiny insectivorous plant quite common in the bog-filled hillsides of Cork and Kerry; and the Irish orchid found in Clare, Galway, and southern Europe.

**CAPE CLEAR BIRD SANCTUARY** Situated on one of the southernmost points in Ireland, Cape Clear Island in County Cork is an ideal place to observe large numbers of rare seabirds. Many of the birds found on the island nest on uninhabited rocks off the coasts of Kerry and County Clare. They fly past the island in their daily search for food, once in the morning on their way out to sea and then again in the evening as they travel back to their nests to roost.

Naturalists travel to the island from all over Europe to observe birds such as Manx shearwaters, gannets, kittiwakes, and fulmars. The bird observatory keeps a record of numbers and types of birds spotted year round.

**Fuchsias growing in the Burren.**

**THE BURREN** An area of about 139 square miles (360 square km) of the coast of County Clare consists of almost bare limestone rock and is known as the Burren. It is not a typically Irish place, having no bogs and few pastures but clean, cracked pavement slabs of limestone, huge boulders, and strangely distorted strata. It has characteristic features—eroded and cracked rocks with sudden sinkholes into which rivers and streams disappear. There are many caves and underground river systems.

The Burren has a reverse temperature curve, which means its hillsides are warmer in winter than the valleys. The rock's stored heat allows grass to grow all year round, providing food for the feral goats that live there. Cattle can also be moved to the uplands to graze in winter.

The Burren offers a poor livelihood to the people living there but has been designated a conservation area. It supports a rare and unusual mix of over 1,100 alpine and Mediterranean-type plants, including gentians, saxifrage, and the rare cranesbill.

**LOUGH HYNE** Lough Hyne is a rare phenomenon in Europe; it is an inland marine lake. It was once a freshwater lake, but as a result of subsidence it is now below sea level. A river connects the lake with the sea. At high tide the sea flows up the river into the lake, bringing in colder seawater and sea creatures, while at low tide the river flows in the other direction, taking warmer waters out to sea.

The effect of all this has been to create a unique maritime environment where certain sea creatures that could not exist in the cold waters of the Atlantic can thrive. Unusual animals inhabiting the lough are red-mouthed goby fish, trigger fish, pipefish, sponges, sea squirts, coral, and luminous jellyfish. The lough attracts researchers from all over Europe who can study creatures that are inaccessible in deeper waters elsewhere.

*Snakes are not found in Ireland. Legend has it that Saint Patrick drove them all into the sea, and they never returned.*

# HISTORY

IRELAND'S FIRST HUMAN INHABITANTS arrived from Scandinavia via Scotland around 6000 B.C. They were hunter-gatherers who spent most of their energies tracking wild animals and collecting berries, grains, and roots.

The Neolithic (New Stone Age) revolution came to Ireland later than to the rest of Europe. Neolithic people grew crops and kept domestic animals. They made pottery and learned how to fashion stone and bone into complex pieces of equipment for digging, cutting, sewing, and woodworking. They created huge dolmens, or tombs, made of enormous stones propped against one another and roofed with a sheet of stone. The position of these tombs, built to face the rising sun, suggests a religion of sun worship. The Bronze Age and Iron Age also occurred in Ireland later than in the rest of Europe, around 1500 B.C. and 700 B.C. respectively. In the Bronze Age, people made elaborate swords and shields of bronze and gold neck ornaments known as torques.

*Left:* **A dolmen in western Ireland.**

*Opposite:* **The 13th-century Record Tower of the Dublin Castle.**

## THE RING FORT

The typical dwelling of the wealthy Celt was the ring fort, or *rath*. Its size and complexity varied with the wealth and importance of its owner. It was built with defense in mind. It stood on high ground and was surrounded by one or two circular banks of earth and stone. The diameter of each embankment was between 50 and 200 feet (15 and 61 m). Sheep and cattle were kept in the ditch between the two banks, and servants and slaves slept there. Inside the inner ring was a large, thatched main building where the head of the household and his wives and children slept. Around the outside of the circle were outhouses, a stone pit for trash, and a cooking area.

Several underground passages, or souterrains, have been found in excavated *raths*. They are thought to have been used for storage during times of peace and to hide people or goods when the *rath* was attacked. *Raths* were the typical country home of the local chieftain well into the fifth century.

## THE CELTS

The Celts were an Iron Age people with their origins in central Europe. Iron was superior to bronze in many ways, and the Celts were able to make better weapons than the tribes that used bronze. Their culture was well established in Ireland by about 150 B.C. and continued to dominate Irish culture for the next thousand years. Their language forms the basis of modern Gaelic.

The Celts were a fierce warrior people. They drove chariots and faced one another in single combat. The dolmens of the earlier people became places of religious significance to the Celts. The typical Celtic settlement was the ring fort, hundreds of which still lie in the fields of Ireland, unexplored and untouched.

## THE COMING OF CHRISTIANITY

Legend has it that Saint Patrick began the conversion of Ireland to Christianity in the fifth century. Saint Patrick established the system of Church government that included bishops and their diocese and encouraged the growth of monasteries. By the eighth century, Irish monasteries had

become European centers of learning. They sent missions to Europe and accepted scholars from all over the continent.

The Gallarus Oratory is a Christian church dating back to the eighth century. It is an example of dry masonry, built without mortar.

## THE VIKINGS

For centuries Ireland suffered attacks from Viking raiding parties. These began in earnest in A.D. 795 against the many monastic settlements around the coast of Ireland. Full-scale invasion took place in 837 and Viking settlements have been excavated in Dublin, Wexford, and Cork. Constant warring continued until the Battle of Clontarf in 1014 when Viking rule was brought to an end. However, many Vikings remained in Ireland, and their culture merged into the indigenous Irish culture.

College Green, a famous park in Dublin, was once a Viking burial ground, and various excavated sites around Dublin have produced Viking swords, ax heads, and spears. The Vikings carried off many Irish treasures as spoils of war, which were found centuries later in grave sites in Denmark and Norway.

The Rock of Cashel in County Tipperary is a pre-Norman monastery.

## THE NORMAN INVASION

The defeat of the Vikings made it possible for Ireland to become a settled society and develop its own culture. Once again the monastic orders flourished, an Irish grammar was written (the first grammar to be written in Western Europe), and art and architecture blossomed.

But despite this cultural renaissance there were still many wars between the various kingdoms. In 1169 the English king, taking advantage of this political weakness, sponsored an invasion of Ireland by Anglo-Norman soldiers. Within 80 years three-quarters of Ireland was under Norman rule. They built stone castles, established a central government, struck a coinage, introduced English law, and in 1297 created a parliament with representatives from each county. Though the Gaelic chieftains lost power, life for the peasant farmer became more settled. Towns were established around the Norman castles and trade flourished.

By the 13th century the Normans had intermarried with the native gentry and had begun to see their interests as Irish rather than Anglo-Norman. However, in 1366 the Statute of Kilkenny prohibited all intermarriage, outlawed the use of the Irish language, dress, and names, and banned all indigenous Irish from entering the walled cities.

## THE TUDORS

Matters changed when Henry VIII (1491–1547), one of five Tudor kings, came to the English throne. He split with the Roman Catholic Church in Rome and created the Anglican Church. His method of rewarding those who supported him was to give them land confiscated from Catholic monasteries. The threat of similar action in Ireland caused a rebellion led by the Kildares in 1534. Henry sent troops to subdue the rebellion, and all Irish landowners were ordered to give up their land to the state. In return, they were given the title of landlord and allowed to carry on as before. This saved Henry the cost of a major invasion of Ireland and kept the Irish lords happy.

There was peace until the accession of Elizabeth I (1533–1603). Under her rule, Protestant adventurers were encouraged to attack Ireland and take away the lands of the Catholic Irish lords. They used as an excuse the conversion of Ireland to Anglicanism, but in reality it was an attempt to gain control over the country. During Elizabeth's reign there were three major rebellions against English rule. Each was followed by the confiscation of land from the local chieftains and the "plantation" of Protestant settlers loyal to the monarchy.

In 1603 the Treaty of Mellifont took half a million acres (200,000 hectares) of land away from the Irish. The land was given to "planters" from Scotland and England who built fortified houses called *bawn* (BORN). Hundreds of Scottish settlers came to the area to take up the land, creating a division between Protestant and Catholic that is still evident today in Northern Ireland.

**Henry VIII, King of England from 1509 to 1547, in a portrait by the German court painter Hans Holbein.**

## THE 17TH AND 18TH CENTURIES

After Elizabeth was succeeded in England by the Stuarts in 1603, the Irish gentry began to hope for a restoration of Catholicism in England and Ireland. During the first of the English Civil Wars (1642–46), both the old Norman families and the Gaelic lords supported the Royalist side.

Oliver Cromwell (1599–1658), the leader of the Parliamentarians in England, was staunchly Protestant and was the man relied upon to impose his faith on Ireland. At the end of the civil war, Cromwell immediately set about the reconquest of Ireland.

Oliver Cromwell, self-styled Lord Protector of England, Scotland, and Ireland (1653–58).

In 1649 thousands of people were slaughtered at Drogheda in the east. Wexford, New Ross, and other towns in the south were also brutally hit. When the Act of Settlement was passed in 1701, the Irish gentry, who had supported the Royalists, were dispossessed of their land, and one quarter of the Irish population was dead.

The Restoration of Charles II in 1660 again raised Irish hopes of a Catholic revival, but despite Charles's religious leanings, this did not happen. His heir, James II, attempted to repeal the Act of Settlement, thus returning all lands to their previous Catholic owners. But before this could take place, James II was himself in flight from the English parliament. He raised an army in Ireland and tried to capture Ulster in the north. In 1690 James's armies were defeated at the Battle of the Boyne.

The rebellion fixed in the minds of the Ulster planters the threat of a Catholic takeover. Catholic soldiers were encouraged to emigrate, laws discriminating against Catholics were passed, and their land was confiscated.

After the establishment of the penal laws, politics settled down for a generation or so. Despite the terrible hardships and sufferings of the Irish peasantry, there were no more hints of rebellion. Gradually, the planters became Irish people with their own interests at heart, just as the Anglo-Normans had done before them.

The American War of Independence encouraged planter feelings of independence. At the same time the success of the Americans made the English government keen to make concessions to the Irish rather than face a second war of independence. Eventually, this led to the peaceful recognition of a very limited form of Irish independence in 1782. Nevertheless the king was still the sovereign, and the Irish ministers of state were still representatives of the British Crown rather than representatives of the Irish people.

## THE PENAL LAWS OF 1695

Under the new laws, Catholics were excluded from public life. Catholics could not vote, join the army, hold public office, own a gun, or own a horse worth more than £5.

Catholics could not buy land. When a Catholic man died his land was divided among all his sons, thus reducing the few remaining Catholic estates into small holdings. If one son declared himself a Protestant he could, however, claim the entire estate. A wife who converted could also claim a portion of her husband's land. If a Catholic tenant made too high a profit on his land he would have the lease taken away.

All Catholic education was illegal, and schoolmasters who broke the law faced fines and imprisonment. Catholic priests were outlawed and liable to be hung, drawn, and quartered if they were caught celebrating Mass. Masses were held in secret in woods or on mountainsides.

*By 1703 Catholics owned less than 10 percent of the land in the country.*

The issue of Catholic emancipation—granting Catholics the right to vote—was taken up by Protestants. The planters, or Ulster Protestants, saw that as long as the vast majority of the population—the Catholics—had no political power, it would always be easy for the British government to reestablish control. In 1778 a law was passed allowing Catholics to buy property. This allowed many Catholic families to move back into Ulster, which was largely Protestant at that time. But emancipation was yet to happen. The British Crown still wielded ultimate political power in Ireland, and too many members of the Irish Parliament saw that their interests lay in loyalty to the Crown and not to Ireland.

The issue smoldered on for several years and was brought to a head in the 1780s by the French Revolution. The people who supported the Irish movement for independence were inspired by the example of the French Revolution. One Irishman, Wolfe Tone, went to France and kept up a continual pressure on the revolutionary government to send aid to the Irish republican movement.

In 1793 war broke out between England and France, and all over Ireland small groups of nationalists began attacking houses and collecting weapons. It was at this stage that the Catholic/Protestant division became important. Alarmed by the prospect of bloody revolution, the planters opposed the rebellion. The French were finally persuaded to send aid in August 1798 and landed more than 1,000 troops at Killala Bay in County Mayo. Organized Irish support for the French never materialized, however, and consequently the French surrendered in September, the rebellion a failure.

The concessions that had been made to Catholics in the previous decades were lost. In 1801 all appearance of Irish independence was erased by the Act of Union that united Britain and Ireland under one king and parliament.

## PEASANT LIFE

After the Act of Union the Irish peasants were just as badly off as they had been before the rebellion. But worse was to come. Peasants rented tiny portions of land at exorbitant prices and paid taxes to the Protestant Church out of what little they managed to earn from their labors. The situation grew more critical as the population steadily increased. In 1841 the population stood at 8 million, about twice that of a census taken at the beginning of the century.

The landlords' solution to this problem was to throw the peasants off the land. Sometimes as a tenancy expired, a large number of peasants living on the land would be evicted and replaced by a single family. The men could find no work so the women and children begged in the street. The situation was at a crisis; it would take only one disaster to make the whole system collapse. This happened with the potato famine of 1845.

*"Their (the Irish peasants') poverty has not been exaggerated: it is on the extreme verge of human misery."*

*—Sir Walter Scott, 1825*

### THE POTATO FAMINE

The potato was the chief crop grown both for subsistence and as a cash crop. Unfortunately, it was particularly susceptible to potato blight, which could wipe out an entire crop very quickly. The crop regularly failed nationwide about every 20 years or so, but the failure that began in 1845 continued until 1849. During this time at least a million people starved to death, while more than a million others emigrated to avoid starvation. Many peasants became too weak to work their tiny farms and more evictions took place. Meanwhile, unaffected crops such as corn sat in grain stores waiting to be shipped to England.

Terrible stories can be told of the dying and suffering that occurred in the workhouses and fields of Ireland in those years and of the deaths in the inhuman conditions of the migrant ships. Many of the passengers on ships bound for the United States died during the voyage. On arrival, more died in disease-ridden camps.

## PARNELL AND THE STRUGGLE FOR INDEPENDENCE

The potato famine gave a greater impetus to the nationalist movement in Ireland. Several years before this, the election of Daniel O'Connell, a Catholic, to the British Parliament had forced Britain to give the right to vote to some Catholic men. In 1875 Charles Parnell, a Protestant, was elected to the British Parliament and led a well-organized movement calling for Irish independence. This movement failed when Parnell was first implicated in some murders and then cited in a divorce case. For a few short years both Catholics and Protestants had again seen independence as their common goal. This was not to last, however.

The bulk of the merchant classes in Ireland were centered in Ulster and were largely Protestant; they were the descendants of the planters settled in Ireland by Elizabeth and James I. As industry began to flourish toward the end of the 19th century the Ulster Protestants saw their future prosperity in terms of remaining part of Britain. At the same time, Irish nationalism was still supported by the Catholic majority. A Gaelic League was formed to promote Gaelic culture and language, and in 1905 Sinn Féin (SHIN fayn), the Irish nationalist movement, became a political party. It was a non-violent party and aimed for political and economic independence from Britain. At this time socialism became another alternative, concerned not with independence alone but with the condition of the peasant classes.

An armored car of the British army patrols the streets of Dublin during the 1916 Easter Rising.

## THE 20TH CENTURY

Ireland entered the 20th century divided by religion, wealth, and political goals and with a living memory of starvation and mass emigration. In Britain things were moving toward acceptance of Irish home rule, a watered-down form of independence. The Home Rule Bill was passed in 1912, but it met with opposition in Ireland. Under the leadership of Sir Edward Carson, the Irish Unionist Party and its offshoot paramilitary organization, the Ulster Volunteers, fought against home rule.

Meanwhile, in reaction to the Ulster Volunteers, the Irish Volunteers was formed. The group was a nationalist force that wanted independence. With the two groups arming themselves, it seemed as if Ireland was headed for civil war. But World War I intervened and the Home Rule bill was postponed. Many republican Irishmen joined the British army in the defense of Britain, convinced that the end of hostilities would see Ireland independent. Others formed secret groups to enlist German help in an armed insurrection.

## THE EASTER RISING

In 1916, in the middle of World War I, while most Irish people waited patiently for the end of the war and the start of home rule, an event happened that took even the mass of the republican movement by surprise. A group of more than 1,000 militiamen from the Irish Volunteers and the Irish Citizen Army marched through the streets on Easter Monday. They ran into the General Post Office (GPO) in O'Connell Street in Dublin, threw out customers and clerks alike, and hoisted the Irish tricolor from the flagpole. Patrick Pearse, one of the leaders of the Irish Republican Brotherhood that planned the uprising, stood on the steps of the GPO and declared the formation of the Republic of Ireland.

The GPO served as the rebels' headquarters. Various strategic points in Dublin were captured, including government buildings, a factory, a college, and other places situated near military barracks. A group tried to occupy Dublin Castle, the seat of government. Various other groups waited in vain for German help to arrive or for uprisings to occur in the rest of Ireland.

Both the British and Irish armies closed in on the rebels and after a bloody week of fighting, the rebellion was over. About 450 people were killed, half of them civilians. Nearly 3,000 others were injured. The leaders of the uprising were arrested and executed.

# WAR WITH BRITAIN

If the majority of opinion both in Ireland and the United States had been against the rebellion, the executions of its leaders changed that opinion radically. In the United States, many Irish Americans were infuriated by the executions and influenced the U.S. government in its decision to enter World War I. The British prime minister saw the need for immediate action. But there was the problem of the Ulster Unionists who were opposed to home rule. A plan emerged to exclude the six counties of Ulster from home rule.

Irish women demonstrate against the execution of the leaders of the Easter Rising.

In 1918 several Sinn Féiners were elected to the British Parliament, but they refused to take their seats. Instead, they formed a provisional republican government a year later, calling themselves the Dáil Éireann, the Irish Assembly. To reinforce the loyalist Royal Irish Constabulary, demobilized British soldiers known as the Black and Tans were moved into Ireland. The Anglo-Irish War thus ensued, with the republicans fighting a year-long guerrilla war against the Black and Tans.

In 1920 the British Parliament passed an act creating separate parliaments, one for the six Ulster counties and one for the remaining 26 southern counties, with both under Britain's authority. In 1921 the Anglo-Irish Treaty was signed. It partitioned Ireland into two—the Irish Free State for the southern counties was established with full self-government rights, while the northern counties remained as part of the United Kingdom. But one group of nationalists, under the leadership of Eamon De Valera (1882–1975), refused to agree to partition and civil war ensued.

Eamon De Valera addresses a crowd.

## AFTER PARTITION

The civil war between the Republicans and those who supported the Treaty ended in 1923. A two-party system evolved consisting of Fianna Fáil (FEEN-ah foil), which constituted the bulk of the Republican forces during the civil war, and Fine Gael (FIN gayl), an opposition party.

De Valera, the man who led the objections to partition, became prime minister, or *taoiseach* (TEE-shock, meaning chief), in 1932 and set up many of the still existing structures of government.

## NORTHERN IRELAND

In 1921 Northern Ireland's own parliament met for the first time. Although Catholics were able to vote, the electoral boundaries were carefully designed to make sure there were no Catholic majorities anywhere. The police force remained largely Protestant. Catholics suffered from poor housing and few job opportunities.

In the 1960s peaceful demonstrations in support of equal rights for Catholics were met with violence from Protestant mobs and the Royal Ulster Constabulary (RUC). In 1969 an annual parade by Protestants led to mass rioting, and Catholic communities barricaded themselves inside their residential districts. The British government sent in troops to protect the Catholics from the Protestants. But this soon turned sour, and the troops who were at first welcomed in the Catholic ghettoes of Derry and Belfast were seen as another arm of the RUC. The illegal Irish Republican

Army (IRA), which was perceived as the Catholics' only defense, organized bombing raids in the cities of Northern Ireland and Britain.

After what came to be known as Bloody Sunday, where 13 demonstrators in Derry were killed by British troops, the Northern Ireland Parliament was suspended in 1972 and replaced by direct rule from Britain. In 1998, after years of bloodshed, the Belfast Agreement (also known as the Good Friday Agreement) was drawn up where all the parties involved in the conflict agreed, some very reluctantly, to a power-sharing government that gave Northern Ireland its own assembly. This lasted until 2001 when Unionist and Republican groups were unable to cooperate any further. In 2003 elections were held for a new assembly and the previously dominant moderate parties on both sides were replaced by more extreme groups opposed to the Agreement.

Catholic demonstrators in Belfast imitate the Fascist salute to ridicule British soldiers, July 1970.

# GOVERNMENT

IRELAND HAS TWO GOVERNMENTS. Northern Ireland is part of the United Kingdom and is represented in the British House of Commons by members of parliament. It also has a fledgling assembly of its own just like any other part of the United Kingdom. The rest of Ireland is an independent republic, with its own constitution and democratic system of government.

The situation is further complicated because a significant proportion of Northern Ireland's population does not wish to remain part of the United Kingdom.

## THE REPUBLIC

The present constitution of the Republic of Ireland has changed little since it was first written. When the constitution was drafted in 1922 during the days of the Irish Free State, it contained an oath of allegiance to the British Crown and recognized the partition of Ireland into 26 southern counties and six northern. The constitution was amended in 1937, removing the oath of allegiance to the Crown but still recognizing the king as the head of the Commonwealth. The Irish Free State was renamed Éire. The constitution originally claimed the six northern counties but they are now omitted. In 1949 the country, without the six northern counties, left the Commonwealth and became the Republic of Ireland.

*Opposite:* **Leinster House, the seat of parliament, in Dublin.**

*Below:* **Members of the Dublin police force help a passerby.**

## STRUCTURE OF GOVERNMENT

Ireland has a president as its head of state although the president has few actual powers. Government is by a two-tier elected body. The Dáil (DHOIL), or lower house, is democratically elected and holds the most power. The Senate is formed by presidential nominees, the prime minister's nominees, and some senators elected from small constituencies such as the universities. The party that holds the largest number of seats in the Dáil forms the cabinet and the leader of the party is nominated as prime minister.

Voting in the Republic is by a system of proportional representation. With five or six parties all vying for votes, negotiations sometimes go on for days after an election. In the case of the 1992 election, it took over two months for a government to be formed while the parties negotiated terms.

Ireland has been a member of the European Union (EU, formerly known as the European Community) since 1973 and has had to alter its laws to meet the human rights demands of membership. But it remains essentially a Catholic state where abortion is prohibited and family planning is highly regulated. Ireland's divorce ban, however, has been overturned since a vote in 1995 approved an amendment (50.3 percent of 1.6 million voters said yes, 49.7 percent said no) permitting divorce. Laws on issues such as abortion and divorce can only be changed by referendum.

## THE NORTH

Attempts to find a way of governing these six counties have been both many and short-lived. In 1922 a parliament and a government were set up in Belfast. Britain retained control of common foreign policy, foreign trade regulation, and the armed forces. In addition, the six counties sent 12 members of parliament to the British Parliament at Westminster. All British laws applied to Northern Ireland.

The system lasted until the deaths that occurred on Bloody Sunday in 1972. *Stormont* (STOR-mont)—the Northern Ireland Parliament—was abolished, and direct rule from Westminster followed. In 1973 a conference of British and Irish ministers was held. The Unionists (who supported union with Britain) and the Republicans (who wanted a united Ireland independent from British rule) in Northern Ireland were consulted, and an executive body was set up that included members of all parties involved. The Unionists, who dominated the workplace, organized a general strike that lasted almost two weeks and brought all activity to a standstill. The executive body was thus abandoned and authority returned to Westminster.

In 1985 the Irish and British governments agreed to allow the Republic a consultative role in the governing of Northern Ireland. In August 1994 the IRA declared a ceasefire, and in October the Combined Loyalist Military Command did likewise, allowing peace talks to begin between all parties. After the Good Friday Agreement in 1998, a devolved assembly for Northern Ireland was set up, but problems over decommissioning of weapons caused it to be suspended. New elections in 2003 brought the extremes of either side into power with little hope of a working agreement.

*Stormont,* the former seat of the Northern Ireland Parliament.

Protestants celebrate the Battle of the Boyne with the July 12 Orange Day Parade, now a symbol of Protestant Unionism.

## NORTHERN IRELAND: THE PARTIES

A major turning point occurred at the 1985 Hillsborough Summit. For the first time, Britain officially recognized the right of the Irish government to have a say in the governing of the North, although the Irish government acknowledged the North's sovereignty. These ideas were formally written into the Good Friday Agreement 13 years later and form the basis for any future peace in the North.

**THE REPUBLIC** From the time that the Irish constitution was written until the Hillsborough Agreement in 1985, the Irish government claimed that it had the right to sovereignty over the six counties. But by its acceptance of a power-sharing role in 1998, it acknowledged that the future of the province was to be determined by the will of the electorate. Ireland is not united in its attitude to the North. In a referendum in the Republic following the Good Friday Agreement, about 94 percent of those who voted chose to endorse the agreement, but there are still strong feelings among a minority that the North should become part of the Republic. The majority of people in the Republic are Catholic, yet there is religious tolerance and little ill will between Catholics and Protestants.

**THE BRITISH** British administrations have dealt with the problems of Northern Ireland in reaction to each crisis rather than with any long-term solutions. They were faced with a terrorist organization, the IRA, that was highly organized and difficult to defeat. After the IRA declaration of a ceasefire in 1994 the British government entered into negotiations with them. This led directly to the process that ended in the Good Friday Agreement and the establishment of a Northern Ireland Assembly in December 1999.

**PARAMILITARY GROUPS** The paramilitary groups in Northern Ireland generally fall into two camps—the Loyalist groups who want continued union with Britain, and the Republican groups that favor a united, independent Ireland.

The biggest Loyalist group is the Ulster Defence Association, a Protestant organization that has killed many Catholics and Republicans. It used to have tens of thousands of members but the number stands at several hundred now. The group declared a year-long casefire in 2003. Other smaller paramilitary groups include the Ulster Volunteer Force and the Orange Volunteers.

The main group on the other side of the conflict is the IRA. In its heyday the IRA controlled many areas of life in the poor housing estates. It is in the process of decommissioning its weapons. However, new splinter groups, disillusioned with the IRA, emerged in the late 1990s, namely the Continuity IRA and the Real IRA. They are still involved in armed conflict.

*"Ecumenism is doctrinally unbiblical ... basically unProtestant ... ecclesiastically unclean ... practically unChristian ... spiritually untrustworthy ... "*

*—Reverend Ian Paisley, outspoken church leader of Northern Irish Unionists*

**POLITICAL PARTIES** In 2004 there were about 15 political parties in Northern Ireland. Most support, in varying degrees, union with Britain or the formation of a united Ireland. A few, such as the Alliance Party of Northern Ireland and the Northern Ireland Women's Coalition, toe the middle ground, promoting themselves as non-sectarian and targeting both Nationalist and Unionist voters.

The Catholic-oriented Social Democratic and Labor Party (SDLP) and Sinn Féin are the two main Nationalist/Republican parties. SDLP is opposed to terrorist activity but has as its aim union with the Republic. It wants to bring about a situation where Catholics no longer see the IRA as a solution to their problems. Sinn Féin, on the other hand, used to be regularly associated with the political violence in Northern Ireland. Sinn Féin members hold the view that the majority of people in Ireland (both north and south) are in favor of a united Ireland and that the minority (the Protestants or Unionists) have no right to impose their views.

The Unionists, meanwhile, see union with Ireland as a threat to their status and well-being. But even within their ranks, there are differing opinions on the Good Friday Agreement. The Democratic Unionist Party (DUP), for example, is against the Agreement and power-sharing. The Ulster Unionist Party (UUP), another major party, is split over the power-sharing issue.

Sinn Féin graffiti in the Falls Road (Catholic) area of Belfast.

40

## THE NORTHERN IRELAND ASSEMBLY

The Good Friday Agreement provided for a 108-member assembly elected by proportional representation. The assembly is led by a power-sharing executive, which is a body made up of members from all the major parties rather than just the party with the biggest majority as in the U.S. and British systems. In addition, several cross-border bodies were set up, including a tourist authority run jointly for both the Republic and Northern Ireland. All paramilitary groups who wished to be a part of the new process had to commit unconditionally to decommissioning all their weapons.

The assembly first sat in 1999 with David Trimble (*left*), the leader of the UUP, as its First Minister and Seamus Mallon of the SDLP as his deputy. Disputes over the decommissioning of weapons caused the Assembly to collapse in February 2000, but it reconvened three months later. The assembly continued to be racked with problems, and in October 2002 the assembly was suspended. By May 2004 it still had not reconvened.

New elections were held in 2003, where the DUP, led by Ian Paisley, received the highest percentage of votes. Paisley refused to deal with Sinn Féin, the second strongest group to emerge from the elections, putting a huge question mark over the power-sharing government provided for in the Good Friday Agreement.

# ECONOMY

THE YEAR 1987 was a watershed year for the Irish economy. It marked a period of harmony between government and industry and trade unions. This was coupled with a rapid growth of the economies of the United States and the European Union. From 1995–2000 the output of the Irish economy grew a world-leading 52 percent, and employment rose from 1.09 million in 1989 to 1.86 million in 2003.

Much of the boom in the Irish economy can be accounted for in U.S. investment (especially in the field of high technology), a jump in women joining the workforce, and huge numbers of returned emigrants and new immigrants. Transnational companies account for the largest proportion of the domestic economy. Irish companies have grown to become transnational, and privatization has reduced the government's role in the economy.

In the boom years, considerable investment was made in the country's infrastructure, which improved roads and telecommunications. But the enormous growth rate of the 1990s is slowing and Ireland has become less attractive to overseas investors as land prices and rents have risen.

A similar boom has occurred in the economy of the North especially with the added security of the new peace. Belfast, in particular, is a more prosperous place with new building projects and greater spending power in the community.

*Opposite:* **An offshore oil rig in County Cork.**

*Below:* **A crystal engraver at work in Waterford.**

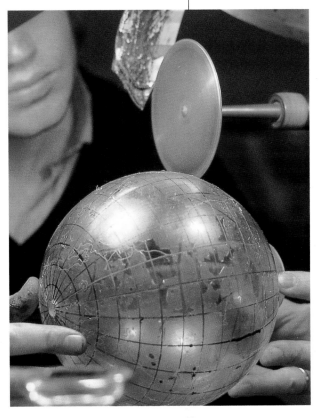

Farmers view livestock at a market in Northern Ireland.

## *FOREIGN INVESTMENT*

In the new Irish economy, foreign investment accounts for almost 92 percent of manufacturing output and 68 percent of the growth in employment from 1991 to 1999. Foreign companies are chiefly involved with computing, precision machinery, pharmaceuticals, data processing, and computer software. Many large multinational firms have invested in manufacturing plants in the country, taking advantage of tax benefits and a highly educated and mobile workforce who are prepared to work at lower rates of pay than in other countries. Most of the growth in employment has been in the major cities, such as Dublin, Galway, Limerick, and Cork.

## *AGRICULTURE*

Since the Republic's entry into the European Union, it has become highly dependent on the dairy industry. Ireland's beef and dairy farms are essentially small-scale businesses with herds of less than 40 cattle on any one farm. The number of farms is slowly decreasing but the ones left are getting bigger—the average size of an Irish farm is now about 79 acres (32 hectares).

In 2002, 7 percent of workers in the Republic and 5 percent of workers in Northern Ireland worked in agriculture. Livestock now accounts for about 90 percent of agricultural output with cattle forming 80 percent of the livestock total. Employment in agriculture has declined since 1997 by about 1 percent per year and it looks likely that this will continue as EU subsidies decline. Most family-owned farms are no longer able to support the family, and small farmers or their wives and children largely find work outside of the farm, tending to farm duties on weekends.

## HORTICULTURE

Ireland's climate, which is mild but wet, means the typical crops of Britain, such as wheat or corn, cannot be grown successfully. Root crops thrive and the potato, which is a staple of the Irish diet, is widely grown. Potato blight can still be a serious threat to the industry and national television regularly gives blight warnings during the summer. Few potatoes are exported because farms operate on a small scale and few have the facilities for packing and processing the vegetable. It is possible now to find Dutch or other European potatoes in Irish shops.

Sugar beet, another root crop, is also grown and forms the basis of a successful domestic sugar-refining industry. In the sugar beet industry the problems of small-scale farming have been overcome by cooperative ventures. Other crops that have been successful in Ireland are mushrooms, which account for more than 20 percent of the total horticultural output, and fruit, such as apples, which are grown chiefly in Northern Ireland.

*Between the Republic of Ireland and the United Kingdom there are no passport barriers, which helps facilitate tourism and business relations between the two countries.*

In 2002 the total catch of fish in the Republic was about 245,000 tons, which was worth 210 million euros ($250 million).

Fishermen inspect their catch in County Cork.

## FISHING

Ireland's fishing industry operates along its western seaboard. Similar to many other Irish industries, it is essentially small scale, with one family owning one boat. In the rest of Europe factory ships catch, process, and freeze the fish, but Irish fishing fleets do not have the technology or equipment. Yet Ireland has the most fertile fishing grounds in Europe. Ireland's waters produce herring, mackerel, cod, whiting, and other fish. But at the moment fishing accounts for only 1 percent of the gross national product. The problem lies in Ireland's fishing quota within the European Union. Ireland's harvest of fish is fixed at the 1973 level when Ireland entered the European Union. Its industry cannot expand and make use of economies of scale. Instead, fishermen have begun farming marine crops, such as scallops and mussels.

## NATURAL RESOURCES

Ireland has few natural resources beyond its fertile landscape. Some zinc and lead are found in County Meath in some of the largest such mines in Europe. Mining is a relatively new industry, and most of the ore is exported in its raw state to Scandinavia.

Peat is Ireland's most valuable natural resource. Many power stations are fueled by peat, and techniques have recently been developed to produce smokeless peat briquettes, which are cheaper and cleaner than coal, an expensive import. The briquettes are used in homes. Peat is now exported to Europe in small quantities.

Ireland's rivers are another valuable natural resource. They are used as a guide for European standards of water purity. Salmon and trout are fished and farmed, and water power is a valuable source of electricity.

**Peat digging in Connemara, County Galway.**

### FORESTRY

Europe has a surplus of beef and butter. While these Irish products sit idly in EU food "mountains," Europe is crying out for timber. Ireland is prime territory for forestry projects. Its climate and soil are highly suitable, but like so many other industries the cost of initial investment is high. The period before any profit can be made is seen as prohibitively long by investors.

About 9 percent of Ireland's land is devoted to forestry projects. It is estimated that Ireland can grow trees in 30 percent less time than, say, Scandinavia. But the profitability of the grass and dairy industries for many years has meant that people have been reluctant to sacrifice good grassland for trees. Now that the European Union is less willing to subsidize the beef industry, trees might begin to be seen as a more profitable investment.

Bushmill's whiskey distillery. Irish whiskey is world famous for its quality and distinctive flavor.

## *MANUFACTURING INDUSTRY*

At the time of the Industrial Revolution, Belfast and Derry became highly industrialized areas with engineering firms, shipbuilders, and their ancillary industries. With the recent decline of the British steel industry, these huge employers have virtually disappeared, and the political disturbances have made the North an unattractive prospect to potential investors. Linen was also a major industry once, but this is now in serious decline, similar to most other cloth-manufacturing areas of Britain.

The Republic of Ireland had little in the way of a manufacturing industry at its birth in 1922. Since then, things have improved to the point where there are many small manufacturing businesses exporting goods such as office machinery and electrical goods to Europe. Distilleries manufacturing Irish whiskey are highly profitable, while the Guinness brewery is known worldwide for its beer.

Ireland has its own national airline called Aer Lingus. It operates services to and from Europe, while a second company leases and services airplanes throughout the world. A railway system operates through both the North and the Republic, and in the last decade major three-lane and four-lane expressways have been built connecting Dublin with the North and the regions.

## TOURISM AND CRAFT INDUSTRIES

Tourism is becoming increasingly important in both the Republic and Northern Ireland. Ireland's unspoiled countryside and rivers with salmon bring many people to the country, while the thousands of architectural landmarks and historical sites are another attraction. Tourist support industries account for much seasonal employment and thousands of small, rurally located "bed and breakfast" businesses depend on tourists to supplement their income from farming. Cork, Kerry, Donegal, Galway, and Clare attract the highest number of tourists.

An example of the beautiful work produced at the Tyrone Crystal Factory in Northern Ireland.

The craft industries of Ireland also depend to a large extent on the tourist market. Throughout Ireland are many small potteries, tweed and knitting firms, and glass manufacturers. The most famous of these, Waterford Crystal, is less important as an employer in Ireland than it once was. In the North, Tyrone Crystal and Belleek potteries are small employers with a long history. Hand knitting is a small craft industry whose fame goes far beyond the shores of Ireland. Donegal hand-knitted Aran-style woollens are exported to the United States, Europe, Australia, and East Asia. It is a growing industry with computer-aided knitting machines adding to the volume of export items.

# ENVIRONMENT

SET ON THE FAR WEST of Europe, Ireland's environment has long been spared the ravages of modern Western Europe in terms of air and water pollution, loss of habitat, urban sprawl, and industrial pollution. This is because for much of the 20th century there was little economic development in Ireland. Its young people emigrated in search of work, international industries avoided Ireland because of high transportation costs and poor infrastructure, others were put off by the political troubles in the North, and native industries could not really take off because the population was small. So Ireland remained a small, rural, underpopulated backwater, its ecosystems, air, and rivers unpolluted by 20th-century development.

That unspoiled rural idyll came to an abrupt end during the 1990s when Ireland experienced an economic boom that earned it the tag of Celtic Tiger. Ireland's industries blossomed, its political problems subsided, and its well-educated and available workforce became a magnet for foreign industries that were looking for an inexpensive base in Europe. EU policies have made farming on small Irish farms economically unviable, leading to intensification in once traditional and sustainable farming practices. With modern machinery and techniques, the outlook for the once environmentally undamaged island has changed.

Ireland now faces many of the problems that took place in earlier decades in Europe. These include urban sprawl caused by a growing population; older industries being abandoned, leaving industrial pollution in their wake; and rural Ireland becoming an unpopulated backwater as small farmers move to the city in search of work. The countryside is increasingly filled with vacation homes that are empty for many months.

*Above:* **Fields in the Wicklow Mountains. The area was made a national park in 1991.**

*Opposite:* **The Glenmalure Valley in County Wicklow.**

**Glass bottles being collected for commercial reuse.**

## GARBAGE

One major problem that has begun to make itself felt in Ireland is waste disposal. In a small, rural country this was not a problem—landfill sites were easily found in some areas while other boroughs burned their waste. But as Ireland's population increased, more and more people began to shop in convenience stores rather than buy locally produced food and goods. So the quantity of garbage to be disposed of has increased enormously. In 1998, 80 million tons of waste was generated in Ireland: 64.6 million tons of agricultural waste and 15.4 million tons of industrial and domestic waste. About 370,000 tons of the waste was hazardous waste, chiefly from industry. In Northern Ireland alone domestic waste has increased by 20 percent in the last decade. In addition, the value of land is increasing and local people object to landfill sites and trash burning.

Ireland has to comply with EU regulations on recycling and has begun to deal with some of its environmental problems quite creatively. In March 2002 a charge was introduced for every plastic bag given out by supermarkets and shops. In just a few months plastic bag usage was reduced by more than 90 percent, and more than 3 million euros ($3.6 million) was raised for environmental projects. Reusable shopping bags are now the norm all over Ireland and this has greatly reduced the amount of rubbish disposed of each week.

Most boroughs in Ireland have introduced a charge for garbage collection. The charge in many cases is based on weight in an effort to encourage people to produce less waste. This has led to some problematic confrontations between residents who refuse to pay the charges and councils who then refuse to collect their trash.

A peat cutter in County Mayo. Peatland accounts for more than 17 percent of Ireland's land surface.

## *ENERGY*

As the economy of Ireland has expanded, its energy needs have also risen. There was a 57 percent increase in its energy consumption between 1990 and 2001. The bulk of the increase was due to increased road use—the number of vehicles on Irish roads surged by nearly 70 percent in the 1990–2001 period. Ireland's energy needs have traditionally been met by imported oil and gas supplemented by indigenous supplies of peat and offshore gas. However, offshore gas supplies are now dwindling and peat bogs are no longer able to supply peat-fired power stations. Peat's contribution to Ireland's total primary energy requirement has dropped from 14 percent in 1990 to 6 percent in 2001, while the country's dependence on imported oil and gas increases yearly. Ireland also has renewable energy sources, such as wind farms.

# LOSS OF HABITAT

A thousand years ago Ireland was densely forested land, covered in broadleaved and conifer trees, the tops of its mountains being some of the few treeless areas. By 1900, with the British Industrial Revolution claiming vast swathes of its forest for building and iron smelting, less than 1 percent of Ireland's land remained forested. Since the 1990s land that had been used for agriculture has been drawn into housing development, leading to more loss of habitat for local species.

Even land still used for agriculture has become less able to sustain local species. The intensification of artificial fertilizer use has led to chemicals leaching into waterways and reducing the number of water plants and other creatures. The destruction of ancient field divisions in order to mechanize farming methods has also reduced habitats. The ancient walls and hedgerows that once provided shelter and nesting places to a whole range of wildlife are no longer available. The use of herbicides and insecticides threatens not only wildflower species but also the beneficial insects, such as ladybugs, which once kept harmful insect populations low. Modern methods, especially the use of artificial fertilizers, have made it possible to support far more livestock on the land than in the past, creating more waste management problems and increased pollution of rivers.

Drastic loss of habitat has also occurred in Ireland's peat bogs. Once covering vast areas of the country, the bogs have been mechanically excavated for peat, which is used as a fuel.

**Trees are felled for timber and other products, and then the area is re-forested. In 2002, 25,000 acres (10,000 hectares) of timber were planted in Ireland.**

## DISAPPEARING WILDLIFE

A resident bird species, once a common sight and sound in rural Ireland, is the corncrake. Corncrakes nested on the ground in hay and cornfields. Crops such as corn have become rare and haymaking, which once took place late in August, has been replaced with silage making in June. Consequently the corncrake's nesting habits have been interrupted by great grasscutting machines that sweep across their habitat, destroying the young and nests. Another fierce destroyer of local species is an introduced animal—the mink. Escapees from captive breeding programs have naturalized in Ireland, creating a new predator for smaller species that take nesting sites previously used by local species.

**THE VARROA MITE** In the late 1990s and early 21st century a new threat to the Irish environment has emerged, threatening all plant life. The varroa mite is a tiny parasite that lives on honeybees. The parasite has already spread throughout Britain, and while it does not kill its host it weakens it to the point where the whole hive is threatened. English and Irish beekeepers have found ways of protecting their bees with chemicals that kill the mite but not its host. However, there is no such protection for the native wild bees of Ireland that the mite also attacks. If native colonies of bees are destroyed, then the plant life that depends on them for pollination is also threatened.

**BADGERS** The badger (*below*) is a native of Ireland, living in earth banks and feeding on small insects and shoots. It is a shy creature that is rarely seen. There are about 200,000 badgers in the Republic and a quarter of that number in the North. The badger has never before posed a threat to any other species. But in recent years the Irish badger population has become infected by tuberculosis (TB). It is thought that the recent increase in bovine TB is due to contact with badgers.

## PROTECTING THE ENVIRONMENT

Air, soil, and water pollution, ever-increasing demands on the land and energy resources of the country, and the additional effects of global warming on a climate that is already subject to the warming effect of the Gulf Stream all put Ireland's environment at risk. But there are efforts in place to protect the environment. An Taisce, for example, is a volunteer group that offers environment-friendly advice and assistance to those who work in the countryside. They also work to protect endangered areas such as hedgerows and mountainsides. The Rural Environmental Protection Scheme operated by the Department of Agriculture and Food offers farmers subsidies in exchange for controlling fertilizer use. It also carries out protective measures such as fencing streams and maintaining hedgerows. The Irish Peatland Conservation Council acts to preserve the rapidly diminishing peatland habitats of Ireland by buying some peat bogs and renovating others. Many of Ireland's peat bogs are protected by EU law.

Few of the lakes along the western seaboard are seriously polluted. The main causes of pollution in Irish lakes are agricultural and industrial waste.

# THE IRISH

WHILE THE REST OF EUROPE was in the Stone Age, Ireland was completely covered in forests and only inhabited by enormous deer whose antlers are still regularly discovered in the bogs. Ireland's first human inhabitants came in boats from Scandinavia. Later, other people arrived, mostly farmers from central Europe.

Celtic culture flourished in Europe in the fourth century B.C. The Celts were driven out of Europe by the Romans but remained at the periphery of Europe, in Brittany (France), Scotland, Wales, and Ireland. The next group of people to influence the Irish were the Vikings, who began with coastal raids and eventually settled in the country. The Anglo-Normans—people originally from France who invaded England with William the Conqueror—were the next wave of invaders. The 17th century saw the arrival of Scottish Protestant settlers, another ancient Celtic race but divided from the Irish Celts through time and by religion.

Other large movements of population have been in the other direction. For centuries, Irish people have emigrated to the United States, Australia, Europe, and Britain. The United States has 34 million people claiming Irish descent. In recent years, however, the number of Irish emigrants has declined, as have the figures for immigrants entering Ireland. In 2003 more than a third of Ireland's immigrants were returning Irish nationals.

*Opposite:* **Children taking part in a folk dancing festival.**

*Below:* **A woman knits an Aran sweater, a traditional winter garment in Ireland.**

## THE ANGLO-IRISH

Many times in Irish history the English sought to gain control of Ireland by establishing loyal subjects in the country. With the exception of those in Ulster, the "planted" families were always landowners rather than peasants. At different times, many groups were known as the Anglo-Irish, but it is those established after Cromwell's time who are currently called Anglo-Irish. Cromwell took land from those who had fought on the Royalist side and gave it to the Protestant soldiers who had served him. The Irish lords were driven west and given new lands.

**Ashford Castle, one of the great stately homes of the Anglo-Irish gentry.**

Ireland today is dotted with huge, dilapidated estates owned by the descendants of the Anglo-Irish. Many of them have been given to the state for forestry or other development. Others are crumbling away, their origins long forgotten and their family names lost to the area. In the 19th century, the Anglo-Irish were prominent in the renaissance of Irish culture. Led by people such as Maude Gonne, Constance Markievicz, and William Butler Yeats, Irish art and literature flourished. Today, families such as the Earls of Lucan and Longford still have their estates in Ireland.

## ULSTER

The word Ulster is now widely used to refer to Northern Ireland. The differences between Ulster and the Republic are obvious. Ulster is more heavily industrialized and urban than the Republic. Its people are divided

Children of Belfast in Ulster.

by religion, with about 28 percent Catholic, 23 percent Presbyterian, and 19 percent Church of Ireland. In the rest of the United Kingdom differences of religion are less important than a nominally common belief in Christianity. In Ulster, religious differences are all-important. Within one small community Catholic and Protestant children may grow up never speaking to one another and are often divided physically by peace walls—high fences that protect the two sides from one another. In the cities, the residential districts are divided strictly according to religion.

The countryside appears to be a little more peaceful and less divided. It bursts into life in July when Protestants celebrate the Battle of the Boyne in which Catholic James II's forces were finally beaten by the Protestant William of Orange. Red, white, and blue banners cover the streets, Union Jacks mark the Protestant homes, and symbols of the Orange Order (a large Protestant organization) are painted on walls. In the estates of Derry and Belfast, huge and sometimes technically superb murals depicting the various icons of the two sides are guarded by the residents.

## *THE WEST OF IRELAND*

In the Republic, the divisions in society seem to be more between the city and the country than religious in nature. The west of Ireland still votes along traditional lines—for Fianna Fáil or Fine Gael, the two parties formed after partition. But the cities vote differently. They want social change rather than any harking back to the old days, and they vote for the parties that represent newer ideas—the Labor Party and the Progressive Democrats, both mildly socialist groups. Ireland's prime minister, Bertie Ahern, is a member of the Fianna Fáil party, which governs in coalition with the Progressive Democrats. There are regular elections in Ireland, most caused by the failure of the parties in coalition to agree on policy.

A small number of Protestant families is all that remains of a social hierarchy where the land was owned by absentee British landlords and administered by loyal and mainly Protestant agents. Prior to independence most of the land in the west of Ireland was owned by the landlords and rented by the peasant farmers. Many of the families now running these farms are descendants of those peasants and have lived on the same piece of land for generations. In the 1970s EU subsidies brought unexpected wealth to these small farmers who then built smart new bungalows beside the crumbling remains of 19th-century farmhouses.

Over the decades, the population movement has been from the west to the cities, or even farther afield to the United States and Britain. The oldest son usually remains on the farm and in many cases does not marry. All over the west of Ireland farms are gradually becoming untenanted or bought up by younger and wealthier neighbors. Eventually, very few large farms will remain and the traditional lifestyle may disappear.

## THE IRISH ABROAD

About 70 million people across the world today have Irish ancestry. The first period of mass emigration occurred during the Great Potato Famine in 1845, and later, many Irish left the country to escape poverty and unemployment.

In 2003 an estimated 20,700 Irish emigrated. About 29 percent of the emigrants headed for the United Kingdom, 22 percent went to other EU countries, 9 percent went to the United States, and the remainder went to other parts of the world.

Wherever they are, the Irish have made an impact on all aspects of life. James Joyce, Samuel Beckett, and William Butler Yeats are all considered to be a part of the English literary tradition. Many star players in top soccer clubs in England are Irish. In the United States, former presidents Andrew Jackson, Woodrow Wilson, Richard Nixon, and John F. Kennedy were all of Irish descent. At least six of Australia's former prime ministers had Irish ancestry. Famous Hollywood actors such as Pierce Brosnan, Colin Farrell, and Liam Neeson are Irish-born.

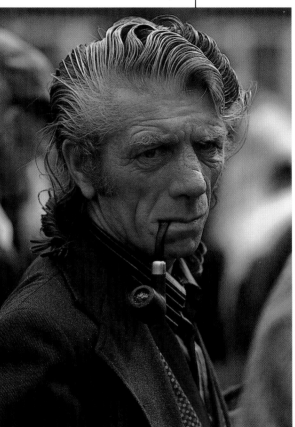

An Irish Romany.

## TRAVELERS

Travelers, or Romany, have existed in Ireland for hundreds of years. Largely gone from the more industrialized areas of Europe such as France and Britain, Romany (once known as gypsies) have survived in rural cultures, especially in Eastern Europe, adopting more or less the language and religion of their country.

The traditional Irish Romany used to be called a tinker and traveled in the distinctive, brightly painted wooden gypsy caravans of the movies, now only seen in heritage centers. Irish Romany earned their livelihood from a number of sources and still do. In the old days, they would have sharpened knives and mended pots and pans, but in today's throwaway, consumer society these services are hardly needed. Another traditional occupation of the Irish Romany was horse trading, and travelers still regularly congregate at fairs and marts selling horses. Modern travelers also trade in antiques, going from house to house buying old furniture and selling it on the roadside.

Two thirds of Irish travelers are now partly settled, still living in trailers but at specially developed sites, some of which have schools, bathing facilities, and electricity. They no longer live in wooden-roofed carts but own large chrome-covered trailers, big enough to be drawn by a truck and sporting many modern conveniences such as gas stoves, satellite dishes, and plumbing. Travelers have always been a marginalized group in Irish society, with their own Romani language, laws, and customs. More recently, their culture has come to be valued and their rights to an independent existence accepted.

## BLOW-INS

The west of Ireland is one of the last areas of unspoiled natural beauty in Europe. Over the years, visitors from Europe and other parts of the world have fallen in love with the countryside and the people. While young Irish people leave their country homes for the city, their places are being taken by disillusioned Europeans. Many of the old abandoned cottages are purchased, along with an acre or two of land, and brought back into use. Their owners raise children, grow vegetables, set up small businesses, and feel grateful that they have found a place where they can escape from the stress of modern living.

Local people affectionately call them blow-ins. The name implies that they have no connection with the land and may just as easily go away again. Many of them do. But others succeed and become as much a part of the landscape as their Irish neighbors.

A subgroup of the blow-ins are the people less affectionately known as hippies. Perhaps happier to call themselves New Age travelers, these mainly young people live in more unconventional communities, often moving from one group to another and practicing alternative lifestyles.

## IRISH HUMOR

The Irish are well-known for their sense of humor, which is often dark and always distinguished by clever wordplay. Famous literary figures, such as Oscar Wilde and George Bernard Shaw, are known for their wit. One classic quote from Wilde is: "I never put off till tomorrow what I can do the day after."

The Irish joke about many things, including religion, politics, and pubs and drinking. On Saint Patrick's Day, many rib-tickling toasts, prayers, and blessings make the rounds. One such prayer goes:

"May those who love us love us,
And those who don't love us,
May God turn their hearts,
And if He doesn't turn their hearts,
May He turn their ankles,
So we'll know them
By their limping."

# LIFESTYLE

COMPARED TO COUNTRIES such as the United States or Britain, Ireland has always been a homogeneous island. Ethnic minorities are tiny and arrived only in recent times. Ireland has remained a place where Christianity is deeply embedded in the attitudes and lifestyle of its people. Political violence aside, there is a remarkably low crime rate, marriage is still the main life choice for most young people, and most people attend church at least once a week. Education, particularly in the Republic, is overseen by the churches.

The traditional family remains the dominant social grouping. With divorce once unobtainable in the Republic and difficult in the North, most people marry for life and remain close to their families all their lives. Even with emigration as high as it has been for a century or more, family ties are maintained for generations after a brother or sister has left and made a new life abroad.

*Left:* **Relaxing in Galway City with a radio and a newspaper.**

*Opposite:* **A group of Irishmen enjoying music and beer in a Dublin pub.**

## THE PUB AND THE CHURCH

The Church was, and still is, the basic medium of social cohesion and interaction in the rural areas. Most people attend church or chapel at least once a week, although the number of young people doing so is decreasing. The service provides people with an opportunity to meet their neighbors and relatives and exchange news. The pulpit not only disseminates shared values but also provides a news service for the parish. The churches organize other social events and maintain support groups, choirs, altar boys, women's groups, and more than one charity.

On Sunday mornings outside the church, the men stand around exchanging views and discussing local news. There is a pub to retire to after the service and before Sunday dinner is ready. But often in Ireland when social issues are raised—as they have been in recent times over divorce, unmarried mothers, abortion, and other contentious issues—the pulpit becomes a focus for debate.

Then there are the ubiquitous public houses of Ireland. They are everywhere and have always provided the chief leisure activity after a hard day's work. Some pubs are as small as a corner in a grocer's shop or the back room of someone's house. They sell coffee and tea as well as alcohol and, like their European counterparts, accept children with a good deal of tolerance.

Most pubs offer at least one night of live traditional music, especially in the tourist season, and listening to music and performing the old ballads is still a part of the Irish way of life. In winter the pub owner will organize card tournaments, darts matches, and other social events. Connoisseurs of the traditional black beer of Ireland (called stout) will spend many hours discussing the relative merits of the pumps and barrels of a particular pub.

It is worth noting that alcoholism is a serious problem in Ireland, with its social life set so firmly in the bars and pubs.

## THE CROSSROADS

Crossroads once held a significance in Irish country life. Without money to spend in the pub or to pay for the dance hall, many young people in Ireland used to spend their weekends at the crossroads where the local fiddler, tin whistle player, or concertina player would strike up a tune and a dance would be held. But few romances were initiated at the crossroads dances. That was largely a matter for the parents and a matchmaker to arrange.

Until recent times, crossroads held another special significance. Traditionally, coffin-bearers would rest at crossroads on their way to the cemetery, and often unbaptized, stillborn babies would be buried there. Now crossroads are just points where two roads cross and cars and trucks zoom past. They have lost their once-held magical status.

Founded in 1592, Trinity College, University of Dublin, is a highly respected seat of learning and can boast as graduates such men of letters as Jonathan Swift and Oliver Goldsmith. Catholics were not admitted into Trinity College until 1873. As a result, Catholic students were for some time denied the best education available in Ireland.

## EDUCATION

In the Republic of Ireland education is compulsory from age 6 to 16. Most primary schools are privately owned. They are administered by the Catholic Church in the case of the Catholic schools and by the Church of Ireland in the case of the Protestant schools. Part of the curriculum in Catholic schools is the preparation for the first holy communion at age 7 and confirmation at age 13.

Pupils go on to secondary education at age 13. After the first three years in secondary school, pupils take a set of national examinations called the junior certificate. At this stage, a minority of pupils leave school to begin their working life. There are several types of high schools: the secondary schools, which teach a traditional academic curriculum and are mostly managed by religious orders; vocational schools, which are non-denominational and emphasize practical skills; and community and comprehensive schools, which have a mixture of academic and technical subjects. Pupils choose which type of school they wish to attend. There are also private schools where students pay fees by the semester.

At 17, there is another set of examinations, the results of which determine whether the pupil enters university or the civil service.

In Northern Ireland, education is administered by the Ministry of Education as in Britain, but here, too, religion plays a much more dominant role than in Britain. Schools are attended by children of the same religion, although there are now inter-denominational

schools. High schools follow the curriculum laid down by the British government, offering about eight subjects of the pupil's choice at General Certificate of Secondary Education level at age 16, and three subjects at General Certificate of Education Advanced level at age 18.

**HIGHER EDUCATION** In the North, about 5 percent of students go on to university, with a larger proportion attending training or technical colleges. Generally, degree courses begin at around age 18 or 19 and last three years. The universities are non-sectarian, although the teaching and administrative staff are mainly Protestant. The universities are often the first place in the North where young Catholics and Protestants meet on an equal footing.

In the Republic, a slightly higher proportion of students attend university—about 8 percent, with around 14 percent in total taking up some form of higher education. Degree courses last four years.

**Schoolgirls at a bus stop in County Wicklow.**

## EDUCATION IN THE COUNTRYSIDE

In rural areas of Ireland where the population density is low, schools are quite small. A typical country school has two classrooms, one for children under age 7 and the other for children aged between 8 and 13. Two teachers would be allocated to the school and class sizes might be very small compared to classes in the cities. A class of 15 children is typical. Often, a child might be the only pupil in a particular age group.

In Ireland, most young people expect to marry.

## LIFE'S BIG EVENTS

**BIRTH AND BAPTISM** For women in the cities, childbirth is as convenient as for women in other Western countries. In the countryside, the unexpected onset of labor can result in a long drive to the nearest maternity unit, perhaps as far away as 60 miles (96 km). Most women have their babies in the hospital.

Religion influences much of the life of the Irish on both sides of the divide. Some 88 percent of the population in the Republic are Catholic, while in the North about 70 percent belong to one or another Christian faith. Whichever the religion, baptism is the infant's first introduction to the Church. The ceremony varies between faiths but involves the ritual symbolic cleansing of the child. The next important moment in the life of the Catholic community is the child's first holy communion. This happens at about age 7 and follows a period of instruction that explains the significance of communion. Children will be instructed by their schoolteacher and the family priest. For 7-year-olds this is a very happy event. The girls wear pretty white dresses that look much like wedding gowns, while the boys usually get new clothes. Friends and relatives celebrate the event.

**MARRIAGE AND DIVORCE** Marriage is the next major event in most people's lives. Secular marriage is allowed in both the Republic and the North but is rare. Mixed marriages between Protestants and Catholics are also possible, but in rural areas they tend to be frowned upon. Men tend to marry in their 30s while women marry in their 20s.

The wedding, which is preceded by an engagement, is usually a big affair. After the church service, a reception is held. The couple stay for the meal and the party that follows, still in their wedding finery, and late at night change into more casual clothes. The honeymoon might be a visit to relatives abroad or a vacation in Europe.

While divorce was not possible until recently in the Republic, there were ways of dissolving a marriage. An annulment that allowed both partners to remarry was possible under certain circumstances. It was only in 1995 that the ban on divorce was voted to be amended.

**DEATH** In the old days, many customs and rituals surrounded the laying out and burial of the dead person. Bodies would be taken out of the house feet first to ensure that the dead never found their way back inside. The coffin would be carried to the cemetery, with the bearers stopping at certain points such as crossroads, which were considered places of magical power.

Making hay while the weather is dry in rural Ireland.

## *LIFE IN THE COUNTRYSIDE*

The population of the Republic is distributed evenly between city and country. In the North, most people live in cities. The rural areas are typically conservative, opposing changes such as the introduction of divorce laws.

Life in the countryside has been changed by Ireland's entry into the European Union. The artificially maintained high prices of beef and milk have meant that a great amount of effort now goes into the production of the commodities.

A farmer's day begins earlier than everyone else's. He gets up at dawn to milk the cows before breakfast. The milk is either put into cold storage for a day or two or taken straight to the creamery.

A creamery is a cooperative agency. A group of farmers share the initial cost of building one. In exchange, the creamery tests, stores, transports, and sells the farmers' produce. The creamery also sells cattle fodder and all the equipment farmers need to run their farms. Each farmer keeps an account at the creamery, and at the end of the month their purchases are set off against their income from the milk. The creamery's profits are divided among the farmers. In the mid-20th century, it was the creameries that made the small farms profitable. Previously, each farmer had to bear the cost of transporting produce and did not benefit from the savings brought about by bulk buying.

Much of people's leisure time in both the country and city is spent with friends or family in the pub.

The church, the pub, and the weekly visit to the local town on market day are the highlights of the farmer's week. Life depends very much on the changing seasons and the weather. In summer, when work gets hectic, each farmer's neighbors will rally round and help bring in the hay. Each man knows that in return for his help, he will get help when he needs it. In winter the supply of milk slows down, and there is time to repair fences and see to all the jobs that were not done during summer. If he has animals to sell the farmer will go to the nearest market town. There the cattle are auctioned off in what appears to be a foreign language but is in fact the fast talk of the auctioneer.

The farmer's wife has a very different life from her ancestors. They washed clothes in the stream, fed the hens and other animals, grew vegetables, kept the fire going, and looked after the house. Now, modern conveniences ease the work, eggs come in cartons, and the central heating is automatic. In many respects life for the farm wife is not that different from a housewife's routine in the city.

**Housewives stop for a rest while shopping in Dublin's O'Connell Street.**

## *LIFE IN THE CITY*

Life in Ireland's cities goes on much as it does in other European cities. In Belfast, there is a rush hour each morning and evening for five days of the week. During the evenings and weekends there is a busy social life in the numerous pubs and clubs.

Life in the southern cities outside of Dublin is a slower affair, but even in the Republic's capital the day begins quite late for most people—most shops and offices open for business at 9:30 A.M. or later. Many businesses close for lunch. Lunchtime will see many people out on the streets, particularly in sunny weather. It is a time for relaxing and meeting friends in one of the many small restaurants and coffee shops that cater to the staff of city businesses. In the suburbs the housewife is a more common sight than in the suburbs of England, where many more women are wage earners than in Ireland. By 3:00 P.M. the children are out on the streets on their way home from school, and things begin to speed up a little as the end of the working day approaches.

## DIVORCE

Being essentially a Catholic state, the Republic of Ireland has passed laws that uphold Catholic values. This has caused some problems since the Republic joined the European Union because some of its laws conflict with EU laws on human rights. Illegitimate children, for example, do not have the same legal rights in Ireland as do children born within marriage.

Divorce laws were voted on in a 1995 referendum, resulting in a margin of less than 1 percent in favor of changing the ban on divorce. An earlier referendum in 1986 showed that many Irish at that time wanted the divorce prohibition to remain. At the time, many people were concerned about the effect a divorce settlement might have on their farm or business assets. Groups opposed to divorce highlighted the fact that the proposed divorce law might allow a farm property to be divided equally between two parties even if before the marriage the farm belonged to only one party. Irish law has not traditionally viewed all property within a marriage as shared, and many people became concerned that new divorce laws might change the status quo. The change in the law to make divorce possible has finally brought Ireland into the realities of the modern age. Thousands of people had been divorced in all but name and had begun new relationships that they were unable to have legally recognized.

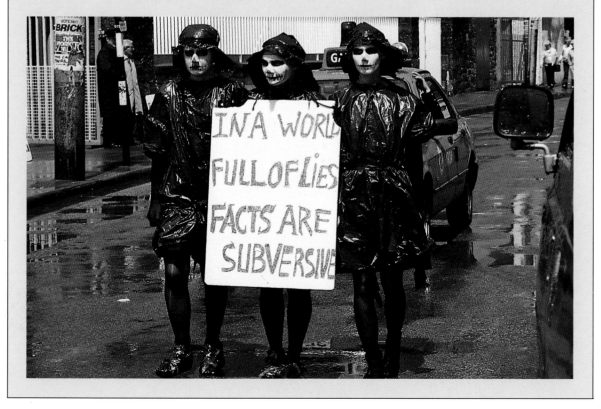

# RELIGION

IRELAND IS A STRONGLY RELIGIOUS COUNTRY, one of the few countries in Europe where religion permeates all aspects of society. In a comparative study made in 1992 in the Republic, Britain, Northern Ireland, and the United States, the strength of religious conviction among the Irish was found to be much higher than among the British. It was, however, close to the degree of faith professed by Americans.

In the Republic, 88 percent of the population are Catholic, 3 percent Church of Ireland, and the rest belong to other faiths or are agnostic. In the North, 40 percent are Catholic, 21 percent Presbyterian, 15 percent Church of Ireland, and 24 percent other faiths or agnostic. In the North, residential districts and whole villages are divided according to religion.

In the Republic, the tiny number of non-Catholics have little voice in a country where the religious beliefs of the majority are enacted by law.

*Opposite:* **Saint Patrick's Cathedral in County Armagh, Northern Ireland.**

*Below:* **In Ireland religion pervades all aspects of life.**

**Ancient Celtic crosses are some of the oldest Christian relics in Ireland and date back 1,000 years.**

## *SAINT PATRICK*

Every Irish schoolchild knows the life history of Saint Patrick (circa A.D. 387–461). He was the son of Romano-British parents who was captured by a Gaelic raiding party and taken as a slave to Ireland. There he lived for six years tending sheep on a mountainside in an area that is now County Antrim. Escaping back to Britain after having a vision where he saw himself leaving Ireland, he was reunited with his family. He was prompted to return to the island by another vision—the Irish calling him back to them. He studied for the priesthood in France, and after he was ordained a bishop, Saint Patrick went back to Ireland sometime in 433. He set up many monasteries and churches.

His mission to Ireland was probably somewhere in the north of the country, as many churches in that area claim to have been established by him. The most notable and most likely is the cathedral at Armagh in Northern Ireland. Armagh is located near an ancient site believed to have been the Celtic capital of the north. Settling there would have been a good idea for a missionary since it was close to the center of power. Saint Patrick's policy was to make friends with the local leaders rather than oppose them with the new religion.

There are many tales about his exploits in Ireland. The most famous tells how he drove all the snakes in Ireland into the sea, thus ridding Ireland of snakes forever. Despite the affection that the Irish have for him, Saint Patrick's Day is a fairly subdued affair in Ireland. On that day the Irish wear shamrocks, which are believed to have been used by Saint Patrick to explain the concept of the Holy Trinity to non-believers.

## *ROMAN CATHOLICISM*

Christianity came to Ireland much later than to the rest of Europe. Legend
tells us that Saint Patrick established Christianity in the fifth century A.D.,
but other missionaries may have arrived in southern Ireland from England
and Europe before him.

Christianity flourished peacefully beside the older religion of the Irish.
As the influence of Christianity grew, the Celtic gods gradually became
heroes rather than deities and the ancient Celtic stories that once illustrated
their godlike qualities became tales of the heroes.

The Irish monks learned Latin, and missionaries were sent to England,
Scotland, Italy, and Gaul (France). The monks had their own methods of
calculating the date for Easter, which many countries followed until the
seventh century. For many centuries after, Ireland's Easter date was
different than that of the rest of the world.

Over time, as an Irish form of Christianity took shape, Latin gave way
to Irish as the medium of education.

## THE MOVING STATUES

In 1985 a strange event happened in the tiny village of Ballinspittle in County Cork in southwestern Ireland. Several villagers passing by a grotto dedicated to the Virgin Mary thought they saw the statue move. Others came the following night and they too thought that the statue appeared to be moving. The news got into the local papers, then into the national papers, and then the international press reported the event. Thousands of people flocked to the small town to watch the statue. Then people in other towns began to report that statues of the Virgin Mary were crying.

The craze for seeing weeping and moving statues spread throughout Ireland until one day, just as suddenly as they had started, the reports about the statues stopped. For some reason, perhaps because of the large numbers of moving statues reported, the events were never treated very seriously.

**CENTER OF LEARNING** From the fifth to the seventh centuries, Ireland was the most significant center of Christianity in northwestern Europe as its monasteries became major places of learning. Some have called this period in Irish history their golden age. Gaelic Christianity, with its own peculiar laws, style of dress, and art developed. Irish history and mythology were recorded, leading to the development of the written Irish language. The elaborate medieval manuscripts of Irish literature were well-preserved and an important source for historians.

The Anglo-Norman invaders who arrived in Ireland in the 12th century were also Christians, so although the Gaelic element of the religion was suppressed, no martyrs were created by the invasion. Ireland's problems over religion began with the split with the Roman Catholic Church in the 16th century under the reign of Henry VIII and the creation of the Protestant Church of Ireland.

The Roman Catholic Church in Ireland has developed the symbols and imagery of the church to suit its own culture. There is a strong belief in the Blessed Virgin Mary, and all over Ireland statues in small grottoes dedicated to her are well tended.

A Catholic priest blesses a car in the Republic of Ireland.

## THE CHURCH OF IRELAND

This is the Irish equivalent of the Church of England, which was created by Henry VIII for largely political reasons. Henry made himself head of the Church and confiscated the wealth of the monasteries to consolidate his political position in England. Differences in doctrine between the new Church of England and Roman Catholicism made the English monarchs' claim to leadership of the Church of Ireland a contentious one.

The Church of Ireland and the Roman Catholic Church are doctrinally close. Both accept the concept of the Holy Trinity, both practice baptism and holy communion, and both are governed by a synod of bishops. In doctrine, the Church of Ireland is closest to the Episcopal Church in the United States, although the latter is more democratic in organization.

On issues such as abortion and divorce, the Church of Ireland is more liberal than the Roman Catholic Church, but its members must obey the laws of the Republic, which are based on the Catholic viewpoint. The Church of Ireland represents a minority of people in the whole of Ireland. More popular, in the North at least, are the other Protestant churches.

A Catholic priest blesses a car in the Republic of Ireland.

83

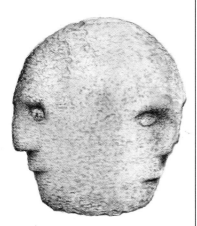

A three-faced idol discovered by a farmer in east Cavan. It dates back to the Stone Age. The Corleck of Tricephalos, as the head is known, is thought to represent Lug the Celtic creator, Dagda the preserver, and Ogma the destroyer. (Coincidentally, the Hindu religion also has a creator-preserver-destroyer trinity.) The Celts worshiped heads, believing they were the center of the human spirit.

## THE PRESBYTERIAN CHURCHES

When England declared itself free of papal authority, England and Scotland were separate countries. Scotland experienced its own Reformation—the revolution that led to the creation of the Protestant branch in Christianity—under the direction of John Knox in 1560. Scottish Protestantism developed its own style, called Presbyterianism.

Essentially, Presbyterian churches are governed along different lines than the Church of Ireland or the Roman Catholic Church, with councils of lay people administering the church as well as the clergy. Both lay people and the clergy preach, but only the clergy can baptize or give holy communion. Ideologically, Presbyterianism is more fatalistic than the other Christian churches; it believes that humanity has little ability to alter its destiny. The Scottish settlers who came to Ireland in the 16th and 17th centuries were mostly Presbyterians and believed it was their mission to convert others. The Presbyterian churches have always accepted the equality of women within the Church, unlike the Roman Catholic Church.

## THE OLDER RELIGIONS OF IRELAND

The religion that Saint Patrick discovered when he arrived on his mission to Ireland is long gone but has been preserved in the folktales of Ireland. The Irish then worshiped a pantheon of gods, both male and female. Druids, an ancient order of priests, officiated between the gods and mortals and had a reputation as men of healing and magic.

Traces of the old beliefs are still to be found in rural Ireland, where the ancient *raths* are referred to as fairy forts. Some people claim that harm will come to anyone who damages one of these rings. "Fairies" is the name in English for the supernaturally powerful people who are said to live in a parallel world that can be entered through certain caves. Fairies can

## KNOCK

On a wet evening in 1879, two women in the tiny village of Knock, in County Mayo, passed the south end of the village church and saw three figures whom they took to be Mary, Joseph, and John the Baptist. They quickly called other witnesses who confirmed what they saw. An ecclesiastical investigation into the event began, and it was declared a miracle. People took their sick children to the church, and it gained a reputation as a place where miracle cures happened. In 1936 another church inquiry confirmed that miracles of healing were happening there.

Knock has now become a place of pilgrimage in Ireland, and the once tiny village has become a major stop on every tourist itinerary of Ireland. An open space outside the church has room for 12,000 people, an airport has been built to accommodate the numbers of visitors, and Pope John Paul II visited the shrine on his tour of Ireland in the 1980s.

move among mortals without being noticed because they are full-size people, not little creatures with wings.

The banshee is a woman of the fairies whose mournful howls can be heard whenever death is about to occur in a family. They are still the subject of much talk, even if no one admits to believing in them any longer.

# LANGUAGE

MANY COUNTRIES that have experienced colonization by another state have seen their indigenous languages and customs suffer. This was certainly true of Ireland where the Celtic language came close to being eliminated altogether. In modern times the language is flourishing but bringing it back into the daily lives of a 21st-century European state is a complex issue. In Ireland, as in other once Celtic regions, language has become a political tool in the hands of the people who want to model the country's future.

The Celtic language, which belongs to the Indo-European group of languages, was introduced in Ireland sometime in 600 B.C., and forms the basis of the language that is called Irish Gaelic.

The Christian missionaries brought Latin to the country and for the first time created an Irish grammar and developed a written Irish language. Borrowings from Latin altered the language; many modern Irish words have Latin roots.

The Vikings also brought new words to the Irish language, and the Anglo-Norman invasion brought Norman-French to Ireland. Each new wave of colonization and immigration affected the language until the English and Scottish began to settle in Ireland.

*Above:* **Road signs in both Gaelic and English.**

*Opposite:* **A crossroads in County Cork.**

# THE IRISH LANGUAGE

Irish or Gaelic was a strong and flourishing language for many centuries after the coming of Christianity to Ireland. Irish scholars learned the Latin of the monks and used the Latin alphabet to write down Irish words. The Latin alphabet had over 20 letters while there were at least 60 sounds in Gaelic, so it was not an easy job. Modern Irish is made even more complex because over the centuries the pronunciation of words has changed while the spelling has remained the same. Learners of Irish must deal with words such as *leabhar* (LYOWER), meaning book, or *gadhar* (GAIR), which means dog.

Irish is an inflected language—the spelling of the words varies depending on how they are used in a sentence. So the Irish word for cat can be spelled *cat, cait, chat, gcat,* or *gcait,* depending on the intended meaning.

The Statute of Kilkenny in 1366 banned the use of the Irish language but was ineffective in achieving this. In the time of Henry VIII, when the conquest of Ireland was consolidated, many Irish lords retained their power only by agreeing to give up the Irish language and culture.

From the time of the Reformation in the 16th century, English policy in Ireland was to discourage the use of Irish in favor of English. When the new Book of Common Prayer—used by the Anglican Church—was written in the 16th century it was not translated into Irish. Irish worshipers were expected to read their new prayers in Latin or English. This alienated the Irish and is one of the reasons why the Reformation had little effect in Ireland and the Church of Ireland has few followers today.

But as English control over the country increased and English became the language of the ruling classes, of commerce, and of learning, Irish developed into a spoken rather than written language. Gradually, Irish

dissolved into dialects that became more diverse as the years passed.

By the time of the Gaelic revival in the late 19th century, people who had begun to produce a written Irish found that no two regions spoke the same form, or spelled the same words in the same way. In addition, many new words had entered the language from English and had no Irish equivalent. The new grammarians had to choose between inventing an Irish word, for, say, bicycle, or using the English one. An invented word sounded foolish, and the English word was resented, so the job of rejuvenating Irish as a modern language was not easy. Even today, there is no government policy in Ireland for new words. Should the word computer be used in its English form or should an Irish version based on Irish root meanings be used? And if an Irish word is invented, which root language should be used? Viking? Latin? Norman-French? Or one of the other Celtic languages such as Welsh?

## THE GAELTACHT

Today, Irish is taught to every schoolchild. A passing grade in Irish is essential for entry into certain universities or the civil service institute. Most young people know some Irish, and many speak it fluently. There are Irish-language television and radio programs, and an entirely Irish television station is possible in the future.

Western Ireland still has many Gaelic-speaking areas where the older people speak very little English. These areas are known as the *Gaeltacht* (GAYL-tahkt) and are carefully preserved as the nucleus around which the language can survive. The Irish government established the Department of Community, Rural, and Gaeltacht Affairs in 2002 to promote the Irish language in the *Gaeltacht*. Various programs and grants are in place to preserve the language and ensure that the younger generation continue to learn it. Irish will never be a language of international communication or of commerce or study, and so its supporters work hard to protect it. The economic trends of Ireland work against this. The good jobs are to be had in the cities (where English is predominant), and outlying areas such as the offshore islands lack facilities of every kind. The young leave the countryside in search of a better life, and only the old remain.

## IRISH ENGLISH

Sometimes known as Anglo-Irish, this is the language that has evolved in Ireland from the English imposed on the people by their English landlords and bishops. It is a curiously poetic language that has somehow adapted to the Irish culture. It has speech patterns found in Gaelic even though for a hundred years many of its speakers knew no Gaelic. It makes use of many Gaelic words that have even entered the English spoken in the United States.

## OGHAM WRITING

It is not quite accurate to say that Irish was not a written language until the coming of Christianity. Gaelic was written down but in a very simplified form. The sounds of the language were represented by a series of grooves and notches cut into the edges of memorial stones, including gravestones. Presumably, the alphabet was also carved into wood, but no examples have survived. Most of the inscriptions that survive tell us the name of the person whose grave is marked and the name of the parents. The inscriptions could not be any longer than this because each letter takes up a large space. Only the corner of the stone could be used, since the alphabet included letters that had to be inscribed on different sides of the stone. Vowels were cut right across the corner; the letters h, d, t, c, and q went horizontally to the left while b, l, v, s, and n went to the right. Other symbols were cut diagonally across the corner. The stone was read from the bottom up. It is estimated that to write a modern novel in Ogham script would take about a mile of cornerstone.

Most of the Ogham stones that have survived are in the southwest of Ireland—largely in County Kerry—but Ogham stones have been found in County Cork, Wales, and the Isle of Man. This suggests that the Irish were colonizing parts of Britain long before their monks went to Britain and mainland Europe as missionaries.

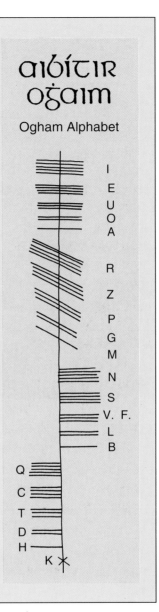

aibítir ogaim

Ogham Alphabet

Gaelic has no words for "yes" and "no." This has had an interesting effect on the English spoken in Ireland, as people avoid using those words. Instead, a speaker will rephrase the verb of the question. For example, in answer to the question "Is this the way to Bantry?" the reply is much more likely to be "It is, so," rather than "Yes."

**Two *boyeens* exploring the Giant's Causeway in County Antrim.**

**STRESS** Another curious thing about Irish English is the way that emphasis is expressed. In British or American English, a meaning is emphasized by stressing one word or another. For example, in the sentence "Are you going to marry Mary?" if we stress the word "you" it means something completely different than if we stress the word "Mary." The first means that we thought someone else would marry Mary, and the second means that we thought he was going to marry some other woman. In Irish English, emphasis is brought about by sentence structure, so the two sentences in Irish English might be "Is it you that's going to marry Mary?" and "It's Mary you're going to marry then?" It would be quite normal for an Irish person to construct a sentence such as "It's to London John is going tomorrow, so t'is." "So t'is" is a kind of confirmation of the truth.

Many Irish words have entered both the English spoken in Ireland and English in general. The suffix *-een*, like the Spanish *ito* or *ita*, is added to the end of words to signify smallness, childishness, or cuteness. The suffix has been added to many Anglo-Irish words, so a small road in Ireland is a *boreen* (BOR-een), meaning lane. Smithereen is a word that has entered the English language from Irish. The word *boyeen* (BOY-een), meaning small or young boy, is common and consists of the English word "boy" with the Irish suffix added.

## YOKES

When an Irish-English dictionary was compiled in 1959, the writers had to confront the problem of how to deal with a proliferation of technical words that had entered the language in the years when Irish was in decline. In various parts of the country items had been given different names. For instance, the writers had 18 different words to choose from for "telescope." It may be that Irish does not render technical expressions very well for the same reason that there are no words for "yes" and "no." These are very specific words that leave no room for the typically Irish negotiation or chat.

A word has entered Irish English that covers all things of a technical nature and somehow sums up the whole technological age. It is the word "yoke." It means anything from a supercomputer to a door hinge. A garage mechanic might point to a wrench and ask his companion to pass over "that yoke," while the salesman for the latest in personal computers might point to the newly designed model and explain it by saying, "Now this yoke over here…" The Irish use the word with a great deal of irony. They know that they are seen in the world, particularly by the British, as simple-minded country folk; every time they use the word they are laughing at both themselves and at the people who choose to view them in this way.

# ARTS

FOR A SMALL ISLAND on the edge of Western Europe, Ireland has contributed a disproportionate amount to world culture. Its writers are world-famous, and its music is known all over the globe.

## *DANCE*

Perhaps the most Irish of all the arts is Irish dance. For generations, Irish people have come together in halls and at crossroads to spend the evening dancing set reels and jigs. The dancing is highly stylized, often with sets of four pairs of dancers dancing in a pattern, changing partners and coming together for a chorus—something like an American square dance. This type of dancing is less popular now. What is more common now is the dance *feis* (fesh). A *feis* is a competition, and the dance *feis* became popular at the end of the last century, when there was an enormous revival of interest in Irish culture.

A dance *feis* is a nerve-racking experience for those taking part. It is largely a competition for girls, although boys also take part. The dancer holds her body rigid with arms fixed at the sides. The virtuosity is in the girl's dancing steps, which are very quick. A limited number of steps are worked into complex patterns of movement while the girl affects an appearance of unconcern with what her legs are doing.

The dresses that girls wear at a *feis* are elaborate and expensive. They are usually green with ornate Celtic designs embroidered on the skirt. Fixed to the shoulders is a short cloak; the rest of the costume consists of white stockings and heavy black shoes.

*Above:* **Girls in traditional dancing costumes.**

*Opposite:* **A fiddler performing at an annual Irish music festival.**

## TRADITIONAL IRISH MUSIC

Irish traditional music is highly creative and inventive. Traditionally, the music was not written down but was composed on the instrument and taught by ear. Even today, the tin whistle—an important element in the sound of Irish traditional music—is taught this way. Because of this, the style of Irish traditional music has been influenced by the capabilities of the instruments used. The two most important instruments in creating the sound of Irish music are the uilleann pipes and the fiddle.

The uilleann pipes are the Irish version of the bagpipes. Unlike the Scottish bagpipes, the uilleann pipes are inflated by a bellows held under the arm. The air goes into a bag that produces a continuous note as background to the melody being played.

**Musicians in a pub playing Irish traditional music on the fiddle, accordion, and banjo.**

## SEAN NOS

*Sean Nos* (SHAN-nohs) singing is a highly stylized form of music. The songs are sung by one person and always in Irish. The songs are like Irish music—the same melody line is repeated continually, each time with tiny variations that the listener must concentrate on. *Sean Nos* singers are different from singers in other Western traditions in several ways. They can close their throat in the same way as you would when about to cough, in order to stop their voice in mid-note. Or they sing in a nasal fashion or change the tempo of their song. Another device is to continue the last note of the line or verse for as long as possible. It keeps the singer in key while she thinks about the next line and has the same effect as the droning note in bagpipes.

The *Sean Nos* songs have local themes. Often, they are about real people or events such as accidents or drownings at sea. The singer sits within the audience, turns away from them, closes his eyes, and cups his hand over his ear to get better feedback on what his voice is doing. *Sean Nos* singers practice the same emotional detachment seen in Irish dancers and musicians.

The fiddle is like the standard violin of Western music, but it is played in a characteristically Irish way. Often the fiddle is rested on the shoulder rather than held under the chin. It is usually played in the first position, covering the range of G below middle C to the B above the treble clef. This means that the fiddler has a smaller range of notes to experiment with, and the left hand is kept freer to move around the notes used. There are slight differences in the fiddle's musical style in the various regions of Ireland.

## POPULAR MUSIC

Some of the biggest names on the contemporary music scene are from Ireland. U2 is one of the world's most popular bands. The group has sold millions of albums and won many awards. U2's songs are politically charged, touching on the Northern Ireland conflict, Third World debt, poverty, and famous civil rights leaders. Another major Irish band are The Cranberries. One of the group's biggest international hits was *Zombie*, which was motivated by the shooting of two children by the IRA.

The legendary singer, Van Morrison, has recorded nearly 30 solo albums. Sinead O'Connor is a critically-acclaimed performer who focuses on alternative and, in recent years, traditional Irish music. Other popular Irish musicians are Elvis Costello, The Corrs, and Enya.

*When Irish people play or sing, the audience takes part in the performance by shouting out encouragement or making funny remarks about the singer or the song. Sometimes a member of the audience will hold the hand of the singer.*

## *IRISH THEATER*

Many famous playwrights whose names pepper the history of English literature have their origins in Ireland. George Farquhar (1677–1707), Oliver Goldsmith (1730–74), and Richard Sheridan (1751–1816) are all of Irish origin. Even more famous names are George Bernard Shaw (1856–1950) and Oscar Wilde (1854–1900), both Irish although their plays do not overtly reflect their origin.

Later playwrights such as John Millington Synge (1871–1909) featured Irish life in their plays. Synge's play *The Playboy of the Western World*—about an angry young peasant who thinks he murdered his father—caused riots when it was first performed in Dublin. Instead of the romantic image of the noble Irish peasant portrayed in Irish plays prior to that time, this play showed the state of Irish rural life in all its rawness and squalor. This was not appreciated by the Dublin intellectuals of the time. Sean O'Casey (1880–1964) followed in this tradition, writing about working-class life in Dublin. Again riots followed.

Modern times have seen the genius of Samuel Beckett (1906–89), an exile from Ireland, whose angst-ridden play *Waiting for Godot* is considered a 20th-century masterpiece.

## IRISH NOVELISTS

Irish novelists are as famous as the country's playwrights. In the 19th century, most English-language writing from Ireland originated in the Anglo-Irish community. Maria Edgeworth (1767–1849) wrote novels about regional Irish life and had some considerable influence on Sir Walter Scott in Britain. Bram Stoker (1847–1912) wrote the novel *Dracula,* which has created a lasting image in Western culture. Two women, Edith Somerville (1858–1949) and Martin (real name Violet) Ross (1862–1915), wrote short stories about Irish life where the Irish peasants figure in as much detail as the landlords in their stately mansions.

The most famous Irish novelist is James Joyce (1882–1941). Born into a large, poor family, he left Ireland as a young man, spending many of his years of exile writing about Dublin. His novels, *Ulysses* (1922) and *A Portrait of the Artist as a Young Man* (1914–15), and his short story collection *Dubliners* (1914) are considered classics of the Modernist genre. His works were disapproved of and difficult to obtain in Ireland for many years. His face was later pictured on the old Irish £10 note.

Brendan Behan (below), boisterous 1950s Dublin intellectual and man of letters, enjoying a beer in a Dublin pub.

## *IRISH LITERATURE TODAY*

Well-known modern Irish writers include John Banville (born 1945), who shot to fame with an award-winning series of books on scientists and science concepts. He has written about 15 books. William Trevor (born 1928) is a decorated novelist and short story writer. Some of the themes in his work touched on the Protestant-Catholic tensions. The Booker Prize-winning author Roddy Doyle (born 1958) writes about the working class in Ireland. Several of his novels have been made into films.

Seamus Heaney (born 1939) is a poet from Northern Ireland who has achieved world acclaim for his poetry. Patrick McCabe writes books and plays, and his most famous novel is a black comedy called *The Butcher Boy*. Women's issues form the theme of writer and screenwriter Edna O'Brien (born 1932).

**Seamus Heaney reading poetry at the Belfast Festival in 1978.**

## W.B. YEATS AND THE IRISH REVIVAL

William Butler Yeats (1865–1939) came from an Anglo-Irish family who lived partly in London and partly in Dublin. As the Irish nationalist movement grew in strength in the late 19th and early 20th century, people like Yeats, who were essentially English in many respects, became inspired with the idealism of a free Ireland. In his poetry Yeats romanticized Irish peasant life, portraying it as noble and strong rather than degrading and poor.

The Revival movement rediscovered all the old Irish customs and honored them in their effort to show Ireland's strong culture. Yeats opened the Abbey Theater in Dublin and put on many plays, some written by himself, about Irish life. It was during this time that Irish was codified into a written language once again, Gaelic sports were encouraged, and Irish words were chosen to replace English ones in important areas. The Irish Parliament of 1922 was renamed the Dáil, the police became the Garda, and Irish kilts, not seen in Ireland for centuries, were again worn. But some people felt that the Irish image created in this movement was too nostalgic and unrealistic, and it was in reaction to this romanticization of the Irish peasant that Synge's play *The Playboy of the Western World* was written.

Yeats's poetry moved beyond the merely romantic, and he is considered one of the greatest English-language poets of this century. He was awarded the Nobel Prize in literature in 1923. In his later years, his political views indicated a sympathy for Fascism, but most people who admire his poetry have scant regard for his politics.

Although Irish literature is alive and thriving, it is ironic that many of the writers who have brought fame and international acclaim to the Republic have found their work banned in their home country because of Ireland's religiously motivated strict censorship laws. O'Brien is one such author; some of her books have been banned for their sexual frankness.

Blarney House in County Cork is a typical example of the Anglo-Irish manor house.

## ART AND ARCHITECTURE

Typical of Irish architecture are the castles of the Anglo-Normans, with their surrounding stone walls and corner turrets. The castles also contain a fortified tower, a gatehouse, and an open courtyard. The main building of the castle is inside the courtyard.

From the 15th to 16th centuries, the typical architecture was the fortified house. This is found mainly around the Dublin area (once called the Pale), where settlers felt the need to defend their houses against the indigenous Irish. A typical fortified house, or *bawn*, consists of a high tower of four or more stories built into a curtain wall. The space inside the wall is an open courtyard. The family lived in the top story of the tower.

The typical and traditional style of Irish house is still in use today. A simple rectangular building, it has a large kitchen with a chimney at one end of the house. In the houses of wealthier Irish, another room was built on to the end, perhaps with its own chimney. This was the parlor and

Many urban Irish live in semidetached housing developments.

would only be used on rare and special occasions. As the Anglo-Irish families were given large tracts of land, they commissioned the building of huge houses, many of which still survive. Castle Coole in County Fermanagh is built in the neo-classical style. All aspects of the house and its furnishings were designed with symmetry in mind. In many places, fake doors were inserted into walls to balance a genuine door opposite. The doors were perfectly crafted, right down to fake keyholes.

At its best, modern architecture seeks to blend in new ideas with the old. One very controversial design is that of the Civic Offices at Wood Quay in Dublin. They are built in a modern style intended to reflect the ancient architecture of Ireland, including the dolmens and round towers of earlier centuries. But there has been much discussion of the buildings, and the next phase of their development—low-rise buildings that might have softened the general outlines—has been abandoned. Dubliners call these buildings the Bunkers.

# LEISURE

THERE IS ONE PASTIME common to all Irish, northern or southern, city or country, English-speaking or Gaelic-speaking: the pleasure of talk. It is a kind of idle chatter, self-mocking and at times fairly incomprehensible to a non-Irish listener. Perhaps because of the country's violent history, big issues are rarely raised in everyday conversation unless agreement is assured in advance. A good example of this is the Republic's national talk show, The Late Late Show, that has been on Irish television since the 1960s. The world's longest-running talk show, it was hosted for decades by Gay Byrne, who put his thousands of guests through some quite challenging talks on Irish life.

A foreigner not used to the importance of "chat" may find it confusing to see the shop owner getting a chair for one of his customers to sit on as she holds up the line at the counter to tell him about her operation.

*Left:* **Talking is an art form in Ireland that few outsiders fully learn.**

*Opposite:* **Youths relaxing at the St. Stephen's Green park in Dublin.**

## *HURLING*

Ireland has several sporting activities that are unique to the island. One example is hurling, a team sport, played with sticks and a soft ball, that has existed in Ireland since history was recorded. In its early days it was a fierce game played by hired warriors. Often, a whole clan became hurlers in the same way that certain clans became poets or fishermen.

Modern hurling is played on a grass field with goals at either end. Each side has 15 players. The hurling stick is wooden and wide enough to balance the ball easily. Players are allowed to raise their hurling stick above their heads and to run with the ball for a few steps. It is a fast game.

Hurling is very popular and is taught in schools in the same way as football or baseball is taught in American schools. Many young men participate in the sport and even more watch hurling matches. Originally hurling was played literally between two villages; the object of the game was to get the ball to the home village. The game lasted until one team succeeded in getting the ball home.

## GAELIC FOOTBALL AND SOCCER

Gaelic football came onto the scene sometime in the 16th century. It is a form of football with 15 players on each team. It is closer to American football than European football, or soccer. The aim is to score a goal between the opposing team's goalposts.

Players can handle the ball briefly, but unlike American football they may not run any distance holding it. To pass the ball, players kick it or strike it with a fist. Tackling one's opponent is a much more aggressive act than in soccer, but the players do not wear the protective gear of American football players.

Unlike the ball used in American football, the Gaelic one is completely round and is slightly smaller than a soccer ball. Just like American football, points are scored both for a goal and for a try—bringing the ball to the goal line.

Soccer, as played in the rest of Europe, is becoming just as popular as Gaelic football. In 1990 the Republic of Ireland team played in the World Cup finals for the first time and reached the quarter-final stage. The team was led by Jackie Charlton as manager who has since remained an Irish national hero. Many in that Irish team played their club soccer in England's domestic league. By the 2002 World Cup there were excellent home-grown soccer players who were stars in England, such as Robbie Keane and Damien Duff. Controversially, a member of the 2002 team, Roy Keane, was dismissed from the squad, which many people believe contributed to the team's eventual elimination in the second round of the competition.

The Republic of Ireland team at the 2002 World Cup in Korea and Japan, just before their match against Saudi Arabia.

*One form of horse racing, the steeplechase, supposedly first took place in Ireland in 1752 when two horsemen called Blake and Callaghan raced each other from the church steeple of Buttevant to the church steeple of Doneraile.*

## HORSE RACING

Horse racing is a national pastime and is treated as both a festival and a sporting event. Many race courses all over Ireland hold races weekly. In addition, Ireland has a calendar of many special events, each lasting from two to four days, which are an amalgam of festival, horse fair, races, drinking, and music sessions. During the festival, the whole town is affected, pubs get a special license to stay open late, music fills every bar, and people while away the evenings playing cards. Huge amounts of money change hands in the betting on the races. From April to September, there are two festivals a month with another two covering the three-day holiday of Christmas. Horses and their riders come from England and farther afield to take part in the races, and many expatriate Irish people arrange their home visits to coincide with one of these events.

The races at Listowel, in County Kerry, in September are probably the busiest and liveliest, since this is traditionally the time when the harvest is completed, and farmers have time for some sport. Another racing spot is Laytown, a seaside resort on the eastern coast north of Dublin; it does not have a festival but its track is unusual. Races are held on the beach while the tide is out. The only permanent buildings marking the race site are the nearby public toilets.

## LEISURE IN THE CITIES

Ireland's cities are tiny compared to places like New York or London, but they have a flourishing nightlife and plenty of activities for people of all ages. The countryside is easily accessible from the cities, and many Irish city dwellers go to the country on weekends. Most city folk have relatives back at the home farm or out in the villages and so visit them regularly. Cities such as Cork, Dublin, and Belfast have all the facilities one would expect of urban areas—bowling alleys, video game arcades, sports centers, golf courses, clubs, cinemas, and theaters.

**Customers in a Dublin pub have a conversation.**

There is a pub to suit every taste and many different types of live music most nights of the week. During the daytime, small restaurants serve inexpensive lunches, but eating out at night is unlikely to be an activity that families can afford on a regular basis. Going out at night in Ireland's urban centers is not the challenging experience that it might be in other cities as it is still relatively safe to walk around at night. Most people spend a lot of time indoors watching television, as do their rural counterparts.

## *LEISURE IN THE COUNTRY*

The countryside has few of the amenities of the city. For generations, country folk in Ireland have made their own entertainment by storytelling, set dancing, and gossip. Now, watching television is also a very popular activity in the evenings.

Ireland is far enough north that the winter nights are long, with darkness falling at about 4:30 P.M. in the middle of winter. Summer is the opposite with daylight lasting until 11:00 P.M. With few street lights outside of the villages, daylight is all-important. Winter nights are spent around the fire, usually a coal and peat fire, watching television. On the weekend, the pub becomes the center of activity in the evenings. Sunday is the usual day for everyone to go out for a drink and discuss events with their neighbors, many of whom are also cousins, or even brothers and sisters. The pubs, like everything else in Ireland, close during the day on Sunday but are open in the evening.

Children have activities organized for them. Perhaps a tin whistle teacher will visit the village to give lessons once a week, or Irish dance or set dancing lessons are organized.

### FISHING

Because of Ireland's proximity to the warm waters of the Gulf Stream and its unspoiled river system, it is renowned for its fishing. Ireland has 8,200 miles (13,200 km) of rivers. Many of Ireland's regular visitors come just for the fishing. Salmon and sea trout live in the sea but breed in the streams, so a salmon fishing industry has its place in the Irish economy. Many people fish for sport and pleasure. Besides salmon fishing, which can be expensive, there is coarse fishing—fishing for the less valuable fish—which is free in all waters. Throughout the year there are many fishing festivals that are mostly tourist-oriented. An avid angler can go from one festival to another fishing during the day and spending the evenings in the pub talking about the ones that got away.

There are bingo sessions on weekends and a trip to the nearest town will provide some kind of live pub music most nights of the week. Larger towns have a movie theater and, if the inhabitants are lucky, a swimming pool or sports center. Restaurants are rare and those that have good reputations will attract customers from miles away. An elegant meal in a country restaurant can cost as much as $75 per person, so trips to restaurants are definitely special occasions.

Since Ireland joined the European Union, many skills of rural Ireland have disappeared. Where 20 years ago a horse plow would have been a common sight, now it is unusual to see any kind of plowing. The farmer's work now consists of fertilizing the grass, harvesting hay for the winter, and tending his herd. But even though it is no longer a part of daily life, many people maintain the old ways for the sheer enjoyment of practicing the older skills. Rural Ireland has many fair days when horse traders, people with cattle to sell, and traveling market stall owners gather in a town. Often on a festive occasion there will be a plowing competition where those who still keep horses show their skill.

# FESTIVALS

THERE ARE THREE major types of festivals in Ireland. Religious festivals cover the main events of the Christian calendar and a few additional saints' days. These are usually quite subdued family affairs. Alcohol is frowned on, pubs are closed, and a visit to church is the main event.

Existing happily beside their Christian counterparts are many very old festivals that precede Christianity. These are much wilder events involving extended hours at pubs, lots of music, and, in summer, lots of tourists.

The third kind of festival is a much more modern and pragmatic arrangement. Ireland gets a lot of its foreign earnings from tourism. Decades ago, people began to realize the earning power of a well organized festival. Now there are countless small festivals all over Ireland, celebrating the mussel harvest, oyster production, the sea, the arts, or some sporting event. Some, such as the Cork Jazz Festival or the big horse racing events, have become enormously successful.

*Left:* **Horse dealers discuss a price for this beautiful specimen.**

*Opposite:* **A woman in Edwardian costume performing at the annual Bloomsday festival.**

## THE CHRISTIAN CALENDAR

Christmas is celebrated quietly in Ireland. In the cities, department stores depend on the period before Christmas to boost their sales, but in the country, the commercialism is more subdued.

An Irish family gathers to pull crackers and eat a traditional turkey dinner on Christmas day.

Most shops and pubs are closed on Christmas Day, which begins with a religious service. The turkey with trimmings is served at around 2:00 P.M., and the remaining daylight hours are spent sleeping or walking off the calories. Recent popular movies dominate the season's television programs and there will be the inevitable 1940s Jimmy Stewart or Bing Crosby movie.

Saint Brigid's Day (February 1) follows Christmas. Saint Brigid is one of the patron saints of Ireland, and on this day people make a *cros Bhríde* (cros VREE-dyuh)—a braided cross made from reeds—on the back of their front door. Saint Brigid is said to look after the hearth fire.

Lent is the next event in the Christian calendar. At the beginning of Lent, the priest anoints the foreheads of his parishioners with ash to remind them of their mortality. In the old days, there would have been dietary restrictions for the 40 days of Lent, but now people make personal decisions to abstain from things such as chocolate, alcohol, or smoking. Easter follows Lent and is a quiet, family affair. Many people from the cities will take this opportunity to visit their families in the country.

## THE ORANGE DAY PARADE

July 12 is the day when the Protestants of Northern Ireland celebrate the Battle of the Boyne. This dates back to the Restoration period of British history when James II began to reintroduce Catholicism to England. The English Parliament disapproved of this and of the heavy taxes he imposed, so it invited William of Orange, James's son-in-law, to replace him. James fled to Ireland where he raised an army and attempted to form a power base in the north. He was defeated by William's forces at the Boyne River, and that event has come to symbolize the final removal of the Catholic threat felt by Irish Protestants.

Unfortunately, in modern times, the event has also become a symbol of the disunity and unhappiness of many Ulster people. Some Protestants use it to express their desire to remain a part of the United Kingdom. Belfast and Derry have Orange Parades where Protestant men, dressed in bowler hats and wearing orange ribbons, parade through the streets. In the past, they would provocatively march through Catholic areas. In recent years, more moderate Protestants have come to see how insulting this can be to Catholics who may have lost loved ones to Protestant paramilitary groups. During July, most towns and villages in the North decorate their streets with banners and symbols of the Orange order.

## FAIRS

**LAMMAS FAIR** The fair is of ancient origin and takes place in Ballycastle in County Antrim on the last two days of August. It once celebrated the time when the first corn harvested was baked into bread. Ballycastle is a small seaside town built in the style of an English village with a town square called the Diamond. During the festival, the square is turned into a fairground with stalls selling crafts and jewelry and sideshows offering pitch-and-toss and other games of chance. Sheepshearing and plowing competitions take place, and musicians entertain on the street or play for a fee in one of the pubs.

A traditional part of the Lammas Fair is the sale of two candies not found anywhere else. Dulse is made from seaweed and is supposed to be good for the stomach. Yellowman is a sweet made from boiled sugar and milk.

**PUCK FAIR** This fair is thought to be pre-Christian and part of a fertility or harvest celebration. It takes place each year in only one place—

Killorglin in County Kerry—and lasts three days. The first day (gathering day) men go out to the mountains and hunt a male goat. The animal is brought into town amid festivities and decorated with tassels, bows, and bells. It is hoisted up on to a high wooden platform in the town square. The goat stays there for the remaining days of the festival and is considered king of the town.

The local pubs stay open longer, buskers (street entertainers) and bands come to the village to play their music, *ceilidhs* are organized, and a great time is had by all. At the end of the three days, on "scattering day," the goat is released and driven back to the mountains while everyone still sober enough comes out to cheer it on.

**The goat is paraded through Killorglin at the Puck Fair.**

***AN POC FADA*** *An Poc Fada* (the long puck) is another event with roots in the mythology of Ireland. One of the ancient Celtic heroes, Cu Chulainn (koo KULL-en), is thought to have walked from his home to the king's palace hitting a hurling ball or puck all the way. In celebration of this myth a hurling festival is held where two hurlers from each of the four ancient provinces of Ireland compete in a competition based on this legend. The competitors cover about 4 miles (6.5 km) of countryside hitting their pucks. A referee accompanies them, keeping score, and an assistant marks the spot where each puck falls. The player who covers the distance in the smallest number of hits is the winner and is declared the successor to Cu Chulainn.

## MODERN FESTIVALS

Many modern festivals are every bit as popular as those whose origins are ancient. The Cork Film Festival and the Jazz Festival (also in Cork) are tremendously popular events bringing world-famous stars as well as thousands of spectators to Cork. The Jazz Festival is often sold out months in advance with every room in the hotels, hostels, and every other kind of accommodation taken. The official events fill every hall and theater in town, while every pub and bar has jazz playing each night. Buskers make a good living on the streets, and the shops and restaurants are busy.

The Rose of Tralee competition held at the end of August in Tralee, County Kerry, is an enormously popular event. Girls of Irish descent from the United States, Britain, Australia, and of course Ireland, attend the festival. Each girl is given an escort for the event and treated to factory visits, a sightseeing tour, and many receptions. The girls are judged over two days in this Irish beauty contest. There is no talk of body measurements, and the girls have to perform a song or dance or play an instrument. The event is televised and for several years was hosted by Gay Byrne, the famous talk-show host whose name is guaranteed to attract a large audience.

The origin of the festival lies in the song, *The Rose of Tralee*. It was written by William Mulchinock, a poet and the son of a wealthy family. He fell in love with a kitchen maid called Mary, but his family forbade the marriage. Later, he married someone else and left the country. There he pined for home and Mary and returned to Ireland. Arriving back in Tralee, he went in search of Mary to discover that she had died. In his sorrow he composed the famous tune.

There are countless other modern festivals. Every small town or village organizes some kind of summer fair. In the North, a successful new venture

Two buskers entertaining passersby at a fair.

is Homecoming Week. The weather in Ireland means that the tourist season is short, usually lasting for only the three months of June, July, and August. Each of the major clans (families) holds events in their town of origin to welcome visitors with Irish roots. Visitors are given assistance to search out their ancestors, and banquets with dancing and music are held.

Another important event in Ireland is Bloomsday, held on June 16. This is the day on which the events of the novel *Ulysses* by James Joyce are set. The novel follows the activities of its hero, Leopold Bloom, and his friend, Stephen Dedalus, around the city. Bloomsday is celebrated by various events such as a trip following Bloom's footsteps around the city's pubs, or a reenactment of some of the scenes from the story. James Joyce was very careful when he wrote the novel; to get the exact details of the streets correct he wrote letters home to his family asking them to check such things as the position of the front door of Bloom's house.

# FOOD

MANY ASPECTS OF LIFE in Ireland have a political significance and food is no exception. For centuries, Irish peasants lived in severe hardship and were malnourished. During the famine of 1845, millions died or emigrated for want of potatoes.

The Irish are acutely conscious of food shortage and hunger and give generously to countries in need of food. According to a CNN news report in 1997, the Irish gave more money, per head of population, to famine relief and other charitable appeals than any other country in the world. The Irish government has helped countries with food shortages such as Ethiopia, Uganda, and North Korea. Hardship and food shortages are still living memories to the Irish, and emigrants returning to the home country well into the 1950s often brought food with them, thinking that the hardships still remained. The situation has of course changed now, especially after Ireland's economic boom.

When eating out in restaurants in Ireland, the visitor notices the quantity rather than the quality. This, too, is related to the significance of food in Irish life. Giving too little food would be very bad for business so very large portions of everything are served, especially potatoes, which are often served cooked in two different ways. A meal without potatoes is a rarity in Ireland.

*Opposite:* **Various types of dessert at a restaurant in Connemara in County Galway.**

*Below:* **A fisherman holding a lobster on Ireland's southern coast.**

**Peeling potatoes for the evening meal.**

## THE POTATO

Legend has it that the potato first arrived in Ireland in the 17th century and was brought to the island's shores by the English explorer, Sir Walter Raleigh. He discovered the vegetable in America and brought it to his estate in Youghal, a town east of Cork City, to see if it would survive. The potato spread in popularity since it requires little tending and flourishes in damp, cloudy weather and peaty soils. By the 18th century, it had become the dominant subsistence crop, to the point where little else was grown for home consumption. The 19th century Irish diet was not good even before the famine. It consisted of potatoes and whatever eggs or milk could be spared. Meat would have been rare on any peasant's table. Potatoes resistant to potato blight are being developed through genetic engineering, while some strains seem to have a natural immunity.

Potatoes are grown commercially in the middle and north of the country and are sold in every corner of Ireland. Increasingly, fewer farmers are bothering to grow potatoes for themselves. Cultivation is carried out by complex pieces of machinery that plant, earth up, and harvest the crop. Potatoes cooked in the traditional way are thrown whole into a huge pot and cooked slowly for an hour. They are served whole and eaten with butter. Another typical Irish food is salted meat. Salting used to be the main means of keeping meat relatively fresh after slaughtering. Salted beef and pork are still favorites even though refrigerators are commonplace. Cabbage is another crop grown easily in Ireland and is a regular part of the Irish diet.

## *THE TRADITIONAL KITCHEN*

The traditional Irish kitchen was the main living room of the house where the family spent the evenings together and where often some of the children slept. A small alcove beside the chimney was built into many kitchens. It was just big enough to hold a bed, and the parents would sleep there with whichever baby needed the most care. The hearth was a huge space built inside the chimney. It was big enough for a chair to be put in beside the fire so that someone could sit inside it next to the fire. Built into the wall of the chimney was a crane that could swing out over the fire or be pushed back against the wall when not in use. Whatever food had to be cooked was hung from this crane, usually in a great iron pot. The pot served as saucepan and oven.

When bread was baked it was put inside the pot and the lid placed firmly over it. Stews and potatoes were cooked in this same pot. At night, the fire was shored up with ashes so that the embers would still be burning the next morning. It is said, quite unrealistically, that in some families the same fire burned for generations.

Somewhere in the kitchen was a barrel filled with salted meat (if any was available), and often scuttling around with the children were hens that provided valuable and easy protein for the family. All the cooking for the family was done over the hearth fire. The fire would heat water drawn from a shallow well for washing and cooking and keep the family warm. Clothes were washed in a nearby stream.

Today, Irish kitchens are equipped for convenience. A modern, solid fuel-burning stove has replaced the open hearth and in a kitchen extension a modern electric stove and a washing machine do the work that was once so arduous. Town kitchens are just as full of labor-saving devices as kitchens in other Western countries.

*Traditional cooked meals in Ireland consist of cabbage, potatoes cooked whole, and meat of some kind. The food is rarely flavored with herbs or spices, except for salt and pepper, and rarely is a sauce or gravy prepared with the meal.*

## MODERN CONVENIENCES

Ireland has gone in for convenience in a big way and with it has come the influence of foreign cuisine. Instant curries, suitably modified to fit the Irish palate, are available, as are Oriental cooking sauces, cake mixes, frozen French bread, low-calorie vegetarian dinners, and so on.

Two or three large supermarket chains dominate most towns. Few small towns have more than one supermarket and it often sells everything from chainsaws to cake decorations. There is also an abundance of seafood in Ireland since people have only recently begun to exploit the rich resources of the sea. Fresh mackerel is everywhere, while scallops and mussels are expensive but guaranteed fresh. Similarly, salmon, cod, herring, and other fish are all locally sold in fish stores.

**A catch of dogfish, one of the many types of seafood that can be caught off Ireland's coast.**

# EATING OUT

Many of Ireland's restaurants serve straightforward and simple food. Visitors can expect a lot of potatoes and a small number of places serving anything other than Western food.

In the last decade or so, some excellent restaurants have opened, mostly by returned emigrants who have trained abroad in big hotels or culinary schools. Most towns have such restaurants, situated far away from the main road and badly advertised, yet always full and with a guest book listing the famous people who have eaten there.

Kinsale, County Cork, site of the renowned Gourmet Festival.

In Kinsale, County Cork, a whole town has dedicated itself to good food, and of its many restaurants 12 have formed a group called the Good Food Circle. Instead of competing with one another for customers they work together, and each year the Circle organizes yet another Irish festival, the Gourmet Festival. It lasts four days in October and consists of food tastings, cooking demonstrations, cabarets, traditional music, and special meals at the various restaurants. In 2002 another annual food festival, the Autumn Flavors Festival of Fine Food and Fun, was started.

Foreign cuisine has in recent years flooded into the city restaurants, especially in Dublin. There are any number of Asian and Asian fusion restaurants serving good authentic dishes. Italian food is particularly popular as is Thai, and many modern restaurants serve an excellent mixture of modern Irish and ethnic food. Outside of the big cities non-Irish cuisine is rarer and more attuned to the blander Irish palate.

## SODA BREAD: A RECIPE

8 cups plain flour
2 teaspoons salt
1 teaspoon baking soda
1 teaspoon cream of tartar
2 ounces butter or margarine
2 cups buttermilk
flour for dusting

Sift dry ingredients into a mixing bowl and rub in butter or margarine. Add buttermilk and mix quickly to make a soft dough. Turn onto a floured surface, knead lightly, and divide in half. Shape each half into a round about 2 inches (5 cm) thick and place on a floured baking sheet. Cut a deep cross on top of each loaf and dust with flour. Bake in a preheated oven (425°F or 220°C) for 25–30 minutes. Transfer to a wire rack to cool. Serve slices spread with butter and strawberry jam.

## *TRADITIONAL FARE*

Besides the cabbage, potatoes, and bacon found in every Irish kitchen, there are other traditional foods in Ireland. One of the best is soda bread—bread traditionally made in the huge, black cooking pot and leavened with baking soda and sour milk. In the old days, it served to use up milk left from the previous day. Soda bread is a flat, heavy loaf but has an excellent flavor. It has largely been replaced with bread made with yeast in commercial bakeries, but many homes and small bakers' shops still produce it.

Another traditional food is brack. This used to be a cake made only during Halloween but is now eaten all year round. It was made from all the things just harvested, but now consists of dried fruit, eggs, lard, and flour.

Carrageen moss is another Irish delicacy, although today it is rarely cooked except to sell to tourists. It is a seaweed that is collected and dried. The dried material is boiled and strained and the liquid left to cool, forming a jellylike substance. It is said to be a very healthy food.

## DRINKS

Probably associated with Ireland more than any other thing is the stout (black beer) originally produced by the Guinness brewery. It is an Irish success story of which all Irish people are proud.

Arthur Guinness was born in 1725 in County Kildare in Ireland. His father was a land steward to a local archbishop and part of his duties was brewing the bishop's beer. The bishop kindly left young Arthur £100 in his will, which provided the finance for the Guinness brewery. At first, Arthur brewed his beer locally, but in 1759 he set out to try his luck and skill at brewing in Dublin. He leased a disused brewery from its owners for many years at an annual rent of £60. He now had in his possession two malthouses for germinating and drying the barley; a mill for grinding the malted barley; a kieve, where the malted barley was mashed up with hot water; a copper, where the liquid was mixed with hops and boiled; and stables and carts for the transportation of the completed brew.

Ireland at that time was the home of stronger stuff than beer, notably whiskey and gin. But porter, a new type of beer, was being imported from England, and Guinness had to decide whether to brew the sour drink known as ale or take on the English rivals. He chose to brew a kind of porter and it caught on. Arthur brewed better stuff than his English rivals: the "extra stout porter" was brewed with a larger proportion of hops to improve its keeping quality. By the turn of the century Guinness's export market was established, shipping mainly to London.

A pub lunch and traditional music accompanied by the inevitable glass of stout.

A dog enjoys his glass of Guinness.

By the 1830s, the British navy was bartering Guinness in East Asia as well as Africa and the West Indies. In the late 19th century Robert Louis Stevenson took a supply with him to the Samoan Islands where he went in the hope of recovering from tuberculosis. In 1909 an expedition to the South Pole took a supply of Guinness. The beer has turned up in literature and on the battlefield. Sam Weller drinks it in Dickens' *Great Expectations*. At the Battle of Waterloo in 1815, an officer wrote home that his wounds were healing more quickly because of his daily ration of Guinness.

As the brewery grew so did the wealth and influence of its owners. They became the typical 19th-century merchant princes and city fathers. The first Arthur Guinness donated generously to the church. The second, his son, became Governor of the Bank of Ireland and supported the emancipation of Catholics. The third Guinness proprietor, Arthur's grandson Benjamin, became a member of parliament, Lord Mayor of Dublin, and rebuilt the city cathedral at his own expense and to his own design. Arthur's great grandson, Edward, inherited the largest brewery in the world, which he modernized and developed to provide model social services for his employees. He also oversaw the listing of the company on the stock market in 1886. He set up the Guinness and Iveagh trusts that provide homes for the poor working class of Dublin and that still contribute to the welfare of 10,000 families. Under his direction, the trusts cleared slum dwellings and built a central market where hygienic conditions could be created for the street traders.

In the old days, the Guinness was brewed at St. James Gate in Dublin. Made from oak, the barrels used to carry the beer had no adhesive or nails. They were so finely made that they did not leak a single drop and were held together simply by the metal bands slipped over the shaped wooden staves. The barrels were at first delivered by horse and cart to the pubs around Dublin or to the canals for their journeys to other towns and, later, to the River Liffey for transportation overseas.

These days, the brewery is a multi-million dollar, computer-regulated, and well-guarded complex still in the heart of old Dublin. Metal casks now hold the beer and huge container ships carry it in vast tanks all around the world.

## POTEEN

*Poteen* (pooch-EEN) is an illegal brew that has been made for hundreds of years in secret places in the Irish countryside. Distilling alcohol is only permitted by government license but the cost of buying legally brewed spirits has always been high because of government tax. Just like their moonshine-brewing counterparts in the United States, people took to making their own brew. Using whatever was at hand, but mostly barley, the distillers set up primitive stills that could quickly be dismantled and hidden should the authorities pay a visit. Like moonshine, the finished product was unreliable but extremely potent. *Poteen* is, of course, still illegal in Ireland, but it is still distilled. Many songs have been written about its effects.

## MODERN IRISH STEW

Irish stew is about as traditional as Irish cooking gets. It is on the menu in most restaurants catering to tourists and in the days before convenience food was on the menu in most Irish households once a week. A good one-pot dish, it would have been cooked up in the old days in the cauldron which hung from a crane over the open hearth fire. This recipe serves four.

2 pounds (1kg) boneless shoulder of lamb,
   cut into cubes
8 ounces (225g) potatoes, peeled and cut into chunks
8 ounces (225g) leeks, cut in coarse slices
8 ounces (225g) scallions

2 fresh thyme sprigs
$1^1/_2$ cups double cream
1 tablespoon butter
Salt
Fresh parsley leaves

Put the lamb in a heavy casserole dish with 5 cups of water and the salt to taste. Bring to the boil and skim off any scum. Simmer for 30 minutes. Add half the potatoes and simmer for a further 30 minutes. Stir to break up the potatoes. Add the rest of the vegetables and the thyme. Simmer for another 30 minutes. Finally, add the cream and parsley and serve with some bread.

# BOXTY

Boxty is one of the many ways of giving a different twist to the Irish staple food of potatoes. It has recently undergone a renaissance in the trendy eateries around Dublin and can now be found with fillings from around the globe. This recipe serves four.

1 pound (500g) peeled, boiled potatoes  
$^3/_4$ cup all-purpose flour  
1 teaspoon baking soda

$^1/_2$ teaspoon salt  
$^1/_2$ cup buttermilk  
2 tablespoons vegetable oil

Cut half of the potatoes into 2-inch (5-cm) pieces. Cook them in boiling salted water until tender, or about 12 to 15 minutes. Drain and mash. Put into a bowl. Grate the remaining potatoes into a small bowl lined with cheesecloth. Squeeze the cloth to remove as much liquid as possible, catching it in the bowl. Add the grated potatoes to the mashed ones, then sift the flour, baking soda, and salt into the bowl. Add the potato starch liquid to the buttermilk and mix well. Brush a large non-stick skillet with vegetable oil and heat it over a medium heat. Drop the potato mixture, a tablespoon at a time, on to the skillet, leaving a little space between each spoonful. Flatten each cake with the back of a spatula, then cook each side until brown, or about three to four minutes for each side. Serve immediately.

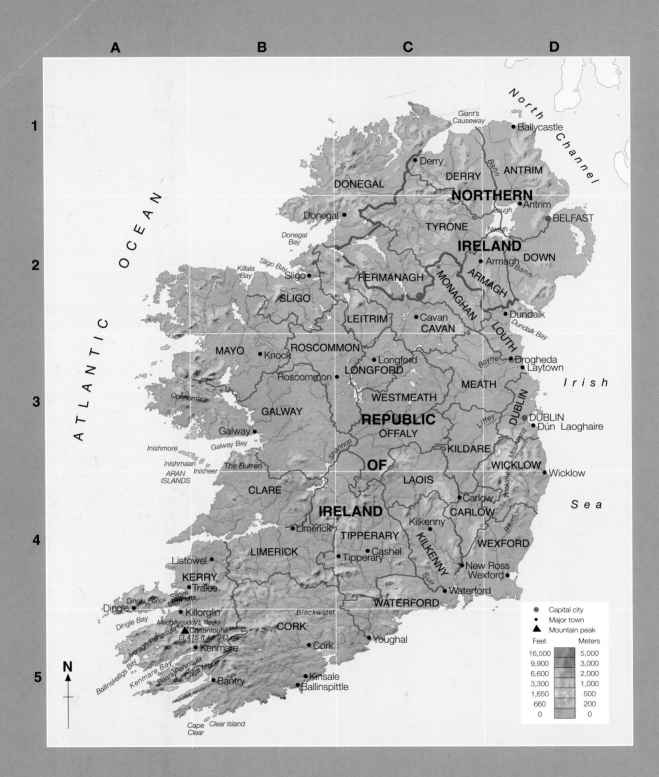

A      B      C      D

1

2

3

4

5

*North Channel*

*ATLANTIC OCEAN*

Giant's Causeway
• Ballycastle
• Derry
DERRY
ANTRIM
NORTHERN
DONEGAL
• Donegal
Donegal Bay
*Bann*
• Antrim
*Lough Neagh*
● BELFAST
TYRONE
IRELAND
DOWN
Killala Bay
Sligo Bay
• Sligo
FERMANAGH
MONAGHAN
ARMAGH
• Armagh
*Bann*
SLIGO
LEITRIM
• Cavan
CAVAN
LOUTH
• Dundalk
Dundalk Bay
MAYO
• Knock
ROSCOMMON
• Longford
LONGFORD
*Boyne*
• Drogheda
• Layton
*Irish*
• Roscommon
WESTMEATH
MEATH
Connemara
GALWAY
REPUBLIC
DUBLIN
*Liffey*
● DUBLIN
• Dún Laoghaire
• Galway
Galway Bay
OFFALY
KILDARE
Inishmore
Inishmaan
*The Burren*
Inisheer
ARAN ISLANDS
CLARE
*Shannon*
OF
LAOIS
WICKLOW
*Wicklow Mountains*
• Wicklow
*Sea*
• Carlow
CARLOW
IRELAND
• Limerick
• Kilkenny
KILKENNY
*Bann*
TIPPERARY
WEXFORD
Listowel •
LIMERICK
• Cashel
• Tipperary
• New Ross
• Wexford
KERRY
• Tralee
*Suir*
• Waterford
Dingle •
*Dingle Pen.*
*Slieve Mish Mts.*
• Killorglin
*Blackwater*
WATERFORD
Dingle Bay
*Macgillycuddy's Reeks*
▲ Carrantouhill
(3,415 ft /1,041 m)
CORK
• Youghal
*Iveragh Peninsula*
• Kenmare
• Cork
Ballinskelligs Bay
Kenmare Bay
*Beara Peninsula*
*Caha Mts.*
• Bantry
• Kinsale
• Ballinspittle
Cape Clear   Clear Island

N
▲

Legend:
● Capital city
• Major town
▲ Mountain peak

| Feet | | Meters |
|------|---|--------|
| 16,500 | | 5,000 |
| 9,900 | | 3,000 |
| 6,600 | | 2,000 |
| 3,300 | | 1,000 |
| 1,650 | | 500 |
| 660 | | 200 |
| 0 | | 0 |

# MAP OF IRELAND

Antrim (county), D1
Antrim (town), D2
Aran Islands, A3
Armagh (county),
  D2
Armagh (town), D2
Atlantic Ocean, A3

Ballinskelligs Bay,
  A5
Ballinspittle, B5
Ballycastle, D1
Bann, D2, D4
Bantry, B5
Beara Peninsula, A5
Belfast, D2
Boyne, D3
Burren, B3

Caha Mountains,
  A5–B5
Cape Clear, B5
Carlow (county), C4
Carlow (town), C4
Carrantouhill, A5
Cashel, C4
Cavan (county),
  C2–C3
Cavan (town), C2
Clare, B4
Clear Island, B5
Connemara, A3–B3
Cork (city), B5
Cork (county), B4–B5

Derry (city), C1
Derry (county),
  C1–C2
Dingle, A5
Dingle Bay, A5

Dingle Peninsula, A4
Donegal (county),
  C1–C2
Donegal (town), C2
Donegal Bay, B2
Down, D2
Drogheda, D3
Dublin (city), D3
Dublin (county), D3
Dún Laoghaire, D3
Dundalk, D2
Dundalk Bay, D2–D3

Fermanagh, C2

Galway (city), B3
Galway (county), B3
Galway Bay, B3
Giant's Causeway, C1

Inisheer, B3
Inishmaan, B3
Inishmore, A3–B3
Irish Sea, D3–D4
Iveragh Peninsula,
  A5

Kenmare, B5
Kenmare Bay, A5
Kerry, B4, A5–B5
Kildare, C3–C4
Kilkenny (county),
  C4
Kilkenny (town), C4
Killala Bay, B2
Killorglin, A5
Kinsale, B5
Knock, B3

Laois, C3–C4

Laytown, D3
Leitrim, B2–C2
Liffey, river, D3
Limerick (county), B4
Limerick (town), B4
Longford (county), C3
Longford (town), C3
Lough Neagh, D2
Louth, D2–D3

Macgillycuddy's
  Reeks, A5
Mayo, B2–B3
Meath, C3–D3
Monaghan, C2

New Ross, C4
North Channel, D1
Northern Ireland,
  C1–D1, C2–D2

Offaly, C3

Roscommon (county),
  B3–C3
Roscommon (town),
  C3

Shannon, river, C3
Slieve Mish
  Mountains, A4
Sligo (county), B2
Sligo (town), B2
Sligo Bay, B2

Tipperary (county),
  B4–C4
Tipperary (town), C4
Tralee, A4
Tyrone, C2

Waterford (county),
  C4–C5
Waterford (town), C4
Westmeath, C3
Wexford (county),
  C4–D4
Wexford (town), D4
Wicklow (county),
  D3–D4
Wicklow (town), D4
Wicklow Mountains,
  D3–D4

Youghal, C5

# ECONOMIC IRELAND

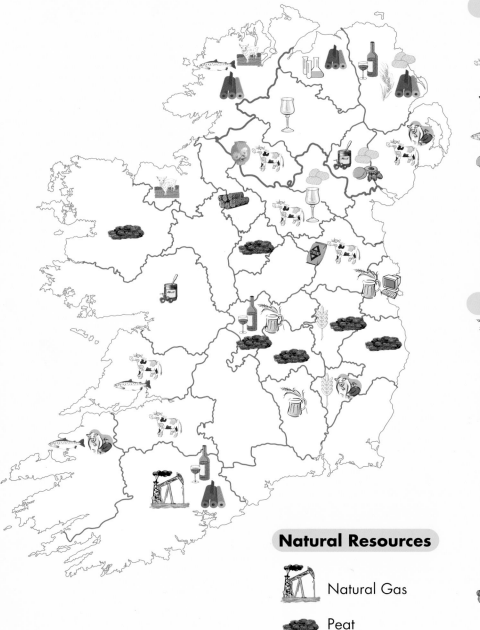

## Farming

- Barley
- Cattle
- Dairy Products
- Fish
- Fruit
- Oats
- Potatoes
- Sheep

## Manufacturing

- Beer
- Cement
- Ceramics
- Chemicals
- Computer Software
- Food Products
- Glass
- Textiles
- Timber Products
- Whiskey

## Natural Resources

- Natural Gas
- Peat

# ABOUT
# THE ECONOMY

## OVERVIEW
Ireland's economy has undergone enormous changes over the past 20 years. In the 1980s it was almost stagnant, highly dependent on agriculture and subsidies from the European Union. The basic agricultural unit was the small family farm. The 1990s saw the emergence of a completely new economy based on IT and pharmaceuticals, and for a decade or so Ireland became the Celtic Tiger, its economy one of the fastest growing in the EU. The turn of the century has seen a slowdown in the economy and the future seems bleak for the remaining small farmers who once supported the Irish economy.

## GROSS DOMESTIC PRODUCT
US$153.4 billion (2002)

## CURRENCY
Republic Of Ireland
1 euro = 100 cents
USD 1 = EUR 0.84 (May 2004)
Notes: 5, 10, 20, 50, 100, 200, 500
Coins: 1, 2, 5, 10, 20, 50 cents; 1, 2 euros

Northern Ireland
1 pound (GBP) = 100 pence
USD 1 = GBP 0.57 (May 2004)
Notes: 5, 10, 20, 50 pounds
Coins: 2, 5, 10, 20, 50 pence; 1, 2, 5 pounds

## GDP SECTORS
Agriculture 6 percent, industry 28 percent, services 66 percent (2003)

## INFLATION RATE
3.5 percent (2003)

## WORKFORCE
1.86 million (2003)

## UNEMPLOYMENT RATE
4.6 percent (November 2003)

## NATURAL RESOURCES
Peat, natural gas, stone, coal

## AGRICULTURAL PRODUCTS
Potatoes, mushrooms, beef, milk, butter, wool, sheep meat, pork products, wheat, sugar beet, barley

## MAJOR EXPORTS
Machinery and transportation equipment, computers, chemicals, pharmaceuticals, live animals, animal products

## MAJOR IMPORTS
Data processing equipment, other machinery and equipment, chemicals, petroleum and petroleum products, textiles

## MAJOR TRADING PARTNERS
Great Britain, United States, Belgium, Germany, Switzerland, Japan

# CULTURAL IRELAND

**The Lake Isle of Innisfree**
Set in Lough Gill on the border of counties Sligo and Leitrim, this is a beautifully scenic area that has been immortalized in a poem of the same name by W. B. Yeats, who grew up in Sligo.

**Carrowmore megalithic cemetery**
A collection of megalithic tombs, standing stones, stone circles, and dolmens in County Sligo dating back to 5000 B.C.

**Galway Festival**
Held every year in July, this is the country's biggest and most popular arts festival when traditional musicians, theater groups, poets, artists, film makers, and classical dancers and musicians descend on the city. The festival is followed by the Galway Races when thousands of people attend the race track for some of the most well-known horse races in the country.

**The Aran Islands**
A group of wild, windswept islands off the coast of County Galway where inhabitants maintain a traditional way of life. Gaelic is the mother tongue of the inhabitants. There are also ancient field divisions and prehistoric sites.

**Skellig Michael**
An offshore island, associated since ancient times with the cult of Saint Michael. It contains the ruins of an early Christian anchorite settlement, including dry stone-walled beehive huts, an oratory, and a cemetery where the monks were buried.

**Lisdoonvarna**
A small town in County Clare which hosts an annual matchmaking festival. In the past, single farmers attended the festival to meet potential wives. The festival now focuses on traditional music and dancing.

**Derry**
A tiny 17th century town with its protecting city walls complete and one of the few late Gothic cathedrals in the British Isles.

**Armagh Cathedral**
Also known as Saint Patrick's Cathedral, the church in County Armagh is the seat of the Protestant archbishop of Ireland and was the center of Christian learning during the Dark Ages of Europe. It is believed that Saint Patrick first established a church here in the fifth century A.D.

**Newgrange Passage Grave**
Dating back to around 3000 B.C., this is an underground room made of stone that housed the bodies of ancient leaders and was possibly also used for religious rituals. Located in County Meath, the tomb has a small opening built into the roof through which a shaft of light illuminates the interior of the tomb during winter solstice. The tomb is decorated with geometric patterns carved into the rock face.

**Trinity College Dublin**
An ancient university founded in 1592 and the place where many of Europe's famous inventors, artists, and scientists studied. It is also home to the Book of Kells, handwritten about 800 A.D. and one of the oldest books in the world. It is a beautifully illuminated manuscript with a Latin version of the Four Gospels. It was illustrated by the monks of St. Columcille Island off Scotland.

# ABOUT THE CULTURE

## OFFICIAL NAMES
Republic of Ireland, Northern Ireland

## NATIONAL FLAG
Republic—Three vertical stripes of green, white, and orange
Northern Ireland—Based on St. George's Cross, with the Crown, the Star of David, and the Red Hand of Ulster

## CAPITALS
Republic—Dublin
Northern Ireland—Belfast

## COUNTIES
Republic—Carlow, Cavan, Clare, Cork, Donegal, Dublin, Galway, Kerry, Kildare, Kilkenny, Laois, Leitrim, Limerick, Longford, Louth, Mayo, Meath, Monaghan, Offaly, Roscommon, Sligo, Tipperary, Waterford, Westmeath, Wexford, Wicklow
Northern Ireland—Antrim, Armagh, Derry, Down, Fermanagh, Tyrone (split into 26 districts based on population)

## GOVERNMENT
Republic—republic
Northern Ireland—constitutional monarchy; the Northern Ireland Assembly was suspended in October 2002 and had not reconvened by May 2004.

## POPULATION
Republic—3.9 million (2002)
Northern Ireland—1.7 million (2001)

## RELIGION
Republic—Roman Catholic 88 percent, Church of Ireland 3 percent, Presbyterian 0.5 percent, others 8.5 percent
Northern Ireland—Roman Catholic 40 percent, Presbyterian 21 percent, Church of Ireland 15 percent, others 24 percent

## LANGUAGES
English, Gaelic

## MAJOR NATIONAL HOLIDAYS
Republic—New Year's Day, St. Patrick's Day (March 17), Good Friday, Easter Monday, Christmas, St. Stephen's Day (December 26)
Northern Ireland—New Year's Day, St. Patrick's Day, Good Friday, Easter Monday, Orange Day (July 12), Christmas, Boxing Day (December 26)

## LEADERS IN POLITICS
Eamon De Valera (1882–1975)—prime minister of Ireland 1932–48, 1951–54, 1957–59
Charlie Haughey (1925–)—prime minister of Ireland 1979–81, 1982, 1987–92
David Trimble (1944–)—leader of Ulster Unionist Party since 1995
Gerry Adams (1948–)—president of Sinn Féin since 1983
Mary Robinson (1944–)—president of Ireland 1990–97
Mary McAleese (1951–)—president of Ireland since 1997

# TIME LINE

| IN IRELAND | IN THE WORLD |
|---|---|
| **6000 B.C.**<br>People first settle in Ireland.<br>**1500 B.C.**<br>The Bronze Age in Ireland | |
| | **753 B.C.**<br>Rome is founded. |
| **150 B.C.**<br>Celtic culture appears in Ireland. | **116–17 B.C.**<br>The Roman Empire reaches its greatest extent, under Emperor Trajan (98–17). |
| **A.D. 300–500**<br>Advent of Christianity<br>**795**<br>Vikings invade Ireland and build settlements. | **A.D. 600**<br>Height of Mayan civilization |
| **1014**<br>The Battle of Clontarf ends Viking power. | **1000**<br>The Chinese perfect gunpowder and begin to use it in warfare. |
| **1169**<br>Anglo-Norman invasion of Ireland<br>**1532**<br>Henry VIII breaks with the Church of Rome. Irish monasteries are destroyed. | **1530**<br>Beginning of trans-Atlantic slave trade organized by the Portuguese in Africa.<br>**1558–1603**<br>Reign of Elizabeth I of England |
| **1600–1700**<br>Plantation of Ireland—Scottish and English settlers are given Irish land.<br>**1649**<br>English forces led by Oliver Cromwell attack Irish towns and massacre their citizens. | **1620**<br>Pilgrims sail the *Mayflower* to America. |
| **1690**<br>William of Orange and James II fight for control of Ireland. James is defeated. | **1776**<br>U.S. Declaration of Independence<br>**1789–1799**<br>The French Revolution |
| **1801**<br>Ireland is brought into political union with Britain, and its parliament is dissolved.<br>**1845–49**<br>The Irish potato famine | |

| IN IRELAND | IN THE WORLD |
|---|---|
| | **1861**<br>The U.S. Civil War begins. |
| | **1869**<br>The Suez Canal is opened. |
| **1912**<br>Home Rule Bill is passed in the British House of Commons but suspended until the end of World War I. | **1914**<br>World War I begins. |
| **1916**<br>The Easter Rising in Dublin | |
| **1919–20**<br>The Anglo-Irish War | |
| **1921–23**<br>Irish Civil War. Ireland is divided into the Irish Free State and Northern Ireland, a province of the United Kingdom. | **1939**<br>World War II begins. |
| | **1945**<br>The United States drops atomic bombs on Hiroshima and Nagasaki. |
| | **1949**<br>The North Atlantic Treaty Organization (NATO) is formed. |
| | **1957**<br>The Russians launch Sputnik. |
| | **1966–1969**<br>The Chinese Cultural Revolution |
| **1972**<br>Bloody Sunday. Thirteen demonstrators are killed by the British army. | **1986**<br>Nuclear power disaster at Chernobyl in Ukraine |
| | **1991**<br>Break-up of the Soviet Union |
| | **1997**<br>Hong Kong is returned to China. |
| **1998**<br>The Good Friday Agreement is signed. | |
| **2000**<br>The Northern Ireland (NI) Assembly meets for the first time. | **2001**<br>Terrorists crash planes in New York, Washington, D.C., and Pennsylvania. |
| **2003**<br>Extreme parties are voted into NI assembly. | **2003**<br>War in Iraq |

# GLOSSARY

**bawn** (born)
A high tower enclosing an open courtyard.

**bog**
Wet, spongy ground which is made up of decomposed vegetation.

**boreen** (BOR-een)
A lane, or small road.

**ceilidh** (KAY-lee)
A form of traditional community entertainment that includes dancing and music.

**Dáil** (dhoil)
The Republic of Ireland's lower house of parliament.

**dolmen**
A tomb made from sheets of stone built into a rudimentary shelter.

**ecumenism**
A movement seeking unity between the various groups and sects within Christianity.

**feis** (fesh)
A competition or festival involving dance and music.

**Gaelic**
The language of the Celtic people.

**Gaeltacht** (GAYL-tahkt)
Areas of western Ireland where the Gaelic language still predominates.

**hurling**
An ancient Irish game played with hockey-like sticks and a soft ball.

**peat**
Compact brownish deposits of partially decomposed vegetable matter found in uplands and bogs and used as a fuel or fertilizer.

**plantation**
A term used to describe the historical settlement of Protestant families in Ireland with the express purpose of creating a citizenry loyal to Britain.

**Sean Nos** (SHAN-nohs)
Stylized form of music sung by one person in Irish.

**Stormont** (STOR-mont)
The Northern Ireland Parliament.

**Taoiseach** (TEE-shock)
Gaelic word meaning chief. The title of the prime minister in the Republic of Ireland.

**Ulster**
Originally the name of an ancient kingdom in the north of Ireland. It now refers to the six Protestant-dominated counties of Northern Ireland.

**Unionist**
The term used to describe the people, mostly Protestant, who want Northern Ireland to remain a part of the United Kingdom.

# FURTHER INFORMATION

## BOOKS

Challinor, Helena et al. *A Beginner's Guide to Ireland's Seashore*. Sherkin Island, Ireland: Sherkin Island Marine Station, 1999.

Corbishley, Mike et al. *The Young Oxford History of Britain and Ireland*. Oxford, United Kingdom: Oxford University Press, 1998.

Cunliffe, Barry et al. *The Penguin Atlas of British and Irish History: From Earliest Times to the Present Day*. New York: Penguin USA, 2002.

Daly, Ita. *Irish Myths and Legends*. Oxford, United Kingdom: Oxford University Press, 2001.

Deary, Terry. *Ireland (Horrible Histories Special)*. London: Scholastic, 2000.

Drinkwater, Carol. *The Hunger—The Diary of Phyllis McCormack 1845–1847*. London: Scholastic, 2001.

Eagleton, Terry. *The Truth about the Irish*. New York: St Martin's Press, 2000.

Johnson, Margaret. *The Irish Heritage Cookbook*. San Francisco: Chronicle Books, 1999.

McCourt, Frank. *Angela's Ashes*. Scribner, 1996.

## MUSIC

Busher, G. *The Croppy Boy*. Gold Sun Records, 1998.

Clannad. *Greatest Hits*. RCA, 2000.

The Chieftains. *The Wide World Over: A 40 Year Celebration*. RCA, 2002.

## VIDEOS

*A Celtic Journey Through Time: A Short History of Ireland*. A & E Entertainment, 1998.

*Eamon's Ireland—A Musical Journey*. Telstar, 1998.

*In Search of Ancient Ireland*. Warner Home Video, 2003.

*Ireland: Land of Majesty*. Renaissance Vision, 2000.

*A Walk Through the Country—Ireland*. Quantum Leap Group Limited, 1997.

## WEBSITES

Heritage Ireland. www.heritageireland.ie

Information on the Irish state. www.irlgov.ie

Irish Examiner Newspaper. www.irishexaminer.com/pport/web/irishexaminer

The Irish Times. www.ireland.com

Irish Tourist Board. www.ireland.ie/home

National Archives Home Page. www.nationalarchives.ie

Northern Ireland Tourist Board. www.discovernorthernireland.com

# BIBLIOGRAPHY

Erwitt, Jennifer and Tom Lawlor (editors). *A Day in the Life of Ireland*. San Francisco: Collins Publications, 1991.

Feehan, John M. *My Village My World*. Cork, Ireland: Mercier Press, 1999.

Grant, Neil. *Ireland*. Morristown, New Jersey: Silver Burdett Press, 1989.

Lalor, Brian (editor). *The Encyclopedia of Ireland*. Dublin, Ireland: Gill & Macmillan, 2003.

Lewis, John. *Ireland: A Divided Country*. London: Scholastic Library, 1989.

Mitchell, Frank and Michael Ryan. *Reading the Irish Landscape*. Dublin, Ireland: Townhouse Dublin, 1997.

Nardo, Don. *The Irish Potato Famine*. San Diego, California: Lucent Books, 1990.

*Northern Ireland in Pictures*. Minneapolis, Minnesota: Lerner Publications, 1990.

Peplow, Mary et al. *Ireland*. Orlando, Florida: Steck-Vaughn, 1990.

Shaw-Smith, David (editor). *Traditional Crafts of Ireland*. London: Thames & Hudson, 2003.

Welch, Robert (editor). *The Oxford Companion to Irish Literature*. Oxford: Oxford University Press, 1996.

Watson, Peter. *A Terrible Beauty*. London: Weidenfeld and Nicholson, 2001.

# INDEX